Home Cooking of India

Recipes from
The Indian Cultural Society of
Urbana-Champaign

ℛ

Compiled and Edited
by
Zarina M. Hock

To Parvati & Rupendra &
extended family,
with love & best wishes,
Govinda &
Rajni
July 22, 2012

© 2012 Zarina M. Hock. All rights reserved.
Editor: Zarina M. Hock
Acquisitions co-editor & consultant: Govindjee
Editorial consultant: Karen Hewitt
Cover photograph: © Shuchi Agrawal
Interior design & layout: Zarina M. Hock
Recipe index: Karen Hewitt
Printed by Martin Graphics & Printing Services, Champaign, Illinois
Published in the United States of America

ISBN 978-0-615-58947-3

The Indian Cultural Society of Urbana-Champaign was founded in 1982 as a pan-Indian organization for members of the Indian community and friends of India in Champaign-Urbana. The Indian Cultural Society's mission is, in part, to promote awareness of India's cultural and social heritage and to raise funds for charitable purposes. (http://icsurbanachampaign.com)

Proceeds from the sale of this book above production and publicity costs will be donated to the Daily Bread Soup Kitchen of Champaign, Illinois. (www.dailybreadsoupkitchen.com)

ॐ
Donors

Publication of this book was made possible by the generous support of the following donors and by funding from the Indian Cultural Society of Urbana-Champaign.

Indra & Narindar Aggarwal
Shyamala & P. R. Balgopal
Pradeep & Ranjit Dhillon
Usha & Rajmohan Gandhi
Rajni Govindjee & Govindjee
Zarina & Hans Henrich Hock
Rashmi & Shiv Kapoor
Jaya & P. R. Kumar
Sharada Panditi & S. S. Kumaran
Nandini & M. A. Pai
Rajeshwari Pandharipande
Padma & Uday Reddy
Umeeta Sadarangani & Marilyn Ryan
Amita Sinha
Vidya & Deoki Nandan Tripathy
Deepa Madhubalan & Madhu Viswanathan

This book was printed at discount by a local business, Martin Graphics & Printing Services, Champaign, Illinois.

The cover was created pro bono by a professional graphic designer who wishes to remain anonymous.

Thank you for your generosity!

Contents

Preface

Like many such projects, this cookbook came about when a group of friends sitting around a kitchen table were chatting about food. We had just eaten a satisfying Indian potluck meal and were exchanging remarks about the dishes we had contributed. Many of us were immigrants from India, who had made Champaign-Urbana our home. Suddenly that magical, high-energy light bulb came on—simultaneously (or so it seemed) in several heads. "Let's do a cookbook for our non-Indian friends in Champaign-Urbana—surely they'd want to try out some of our recipes."

A flimsy straw poll suggests that we could be right. We'll find out soon enough. We offer this informal collection to the C-U community in the hope that you will enjoy making some of those foods that you have eaten in our homes. Many of these recipes come from our mothers' kitchens in India, and we have adapted them to our new homeland. Some were simply made up in a kitchen in Champaign-Urbana as we adjusted to our new environment. Still others are unabashedly fusion foods.

Whatever their evolution, these dishes represent our way of life in this diverse and welcoming community— one that has embraced us and one that we now call home. And that is something to celebrate.

And finally, our project was also undertaken to reaffirm in part the mission of the Indian Cultural Society, which includes fundraising for charitable purposes, participation in activities that connect the Indian community with the wider community, and a sharing of our culture. It is, then, with joy that we present through sales of this book an offering to the Daily Bread Soup Kitchen, whose work in our community is truly inspiring.

ಬಿ Zarina Hock ಝ

Acknowledgments

This project was a long time in the making because, like all recently retired individuals, I got pulled into more community activities than I could juggle. And, reeling in those recipes and calling on promises made at parties took more time than I had realized when I made my commitment.

Many people must be thanked, Govindjee in particular, who despite his inordinately busy life as Professor Emeritus of Biochemistry, Biophysics and Plant Biology, made it his mission to help me collect recipes and to encourage me (often giving me a friendly push). His dedication to the Indian Cultural Society has been inspiring, and his fundraising efforts to underwrite this project nothing short of extraordinary. How he made the time to do this, along with his research, publishing, conference participation, and traveling is simple—he's the professor who doesn't sleep.

To those members of the community who shared their recipes with me: thank you, thank you. Whether dictated on the phone, e-mailed, or scribbled on a napkin at a party, your recipes gave us the range and variety we needed. You were patient with my questions and generous with your recipes.

Shuchi Agrawal ungrudgingly contributed her recipes and helped with publicity. Shuchi, who describes herself as a foodie, is an accomplished cook whose website, www.chezshuchi.com, features Indian vegetarian cuisine and other foods. Her culinary interest started when she was residing in France. A rich resource, *ChezShuchi* offers recipes in English and Hindi, accompanied by fabulous photographs of preparatory steps and finished products. Shuchi has presented cooking demonstrations both locally and in France. She also supplied the photograph, which a professional graphic designer used for the cover. The picture of Shuchi's Diwali dinner table was a perfect fit for this publication.

Tulsi Dharmarajan, a former resident of Champaign, allowed me to cherry-pick recipes from her blog, http://tulsid.wordpress. com/ category/food/. Kavitha Reddy graciously granted us permission to reprint recipes from her publication, *The Indian Soy Cookbook*. I mined (with permission) the UIUC Linguistics Department's decades-old International Linguistic Gourmet Cookbooks for a few excellent recipes by contributors who are still in our community and who offered additional recipes as well.

I'm especially grateful to Manisha Bhagwat, who read the manuscript and advised me on content, and to Margrith Mistry, whose finely honed skills as proofreader helped catch my many keyboarding errors. Nutrition Consultant Vijaya Jain took time from her international commitments to share some thoughts about Indian cuisine. Mukesh Kukreti worked hard to acquire advertisements to underwrite production costs. My warmest thanks to them all.

Above all, I am indebted to Karen Hewitt, a cookbook editor and publishing professional, who appeared magically in my life during the editing process and volunteered the wealth of her expertise. She also created the recipe index when I despaired of completing this project. I learned much from her invaluable insights and critiques, offered with tact and generosity.

And much gratitude to my husband Hans Henrich who advised, tasted, critiqued, and contributed recipes (yes indeed, a German can cook Indian food) and who also unraveled for me Microsoft Word's mysteries of page design. For a Mac man that was a magnanimous gesture. He also amiably put up with me during what seemed to be an interminable process.

Introduction

India is a land of enormous diversity, a country where every region has distinctive languages, music, artistic and literary traditions, styles of dress, handicrafts, and, yes, foods. To be Indian is to enjoy this diversity—it is something we celebrate, cultivate, joke about, take pride in, and assume as integral to life. This informal collection of recipes, offered by the Indian Cultural Society of Urbana-Champaign, mirrors the diversity of Indian foods, some simple and some elaborate. More than that, it provides recipes adapted to local (Midwest) conditions, as well as traditional ones from the Indian Subcontinent. As with the foods of all countries, volumes have been written and continue to be produced about Indian cuisine. This book—a community's collection of home cooking—is necessarily modest, but it represents foods eaten by families in Champaign-Urbana. Authentic and diverse.

An Ancient Food Tradition

You will notice a wide range of vegetarian dishes in this book. Although certainly not exclusively vegetarian, India has a large population that does not eat meat, as well as a long and venerated tradition of vegetarian cooking. Vegetables are never considered merely a supplement to a main, meat-based meal. Vegetable proteins are recognized as nutritious alternatives to meat, and it is completely acceptable to serve an extravagant, tasty, and richly varied meal without any meat products. As one Time-Life cookbook writer, Santha Rama Rau, puts it, "India has produced one of the most varied and imaginative vegetarian cuisines in the world." Vijaya Jain's comments after this introduction give you a glimpse into the basis of this ancient food tradition.

The following notes are intended to help orient you if you are unfamiliar with Indian cooking—all small matters, easily negotiated, adapted, and some even ignored.

9

Transliteration of Names

I have used the common, everyday transliteration used in India. My method lays no claim to linguistic consistency but is generally understood by those from India or familiar with English in India (translations are, however, provided). One sees such transliterations routinely on billboards, newspapers, and other printed material. It causes my linguist husband much despair; he would prefer the usage of a Sanskrit scholar. He has learned, however, to live with the inconsistencies. So if he can, I hope you will.

Weights and Measures

Since recipes were solicited informally, some of the measures were, when submitted, informal too—a pinch of this, a handful of that, and so on. Others were metric; many were standard American; and some—well—nonexistent. With the patient cooperation of the contributors and the help of web conversion tables, I have tried to render the measurements in standard American kitchen usage. Adjust the quantities as you try out the recipes.

Terminology

The names of most dishes are given in English translation, with Indian names in parentheses. To Indian readers (and I hope there will be some), these translations may sound strange or quaint, but my intent here is to make the book as accessible as possible.

In the recipes' ingredient lists, however, I've done the opposite with some items. That is because when looking for them in the store, you are more likely to find these products with their Indian names only. Besides, many of the ingredients appear so frequently that you may as well become familiar with them, for example, *amchur, basmati rice, curry leaves, dal, hing* (so much easier to spell than *asafoetida*), *jeera/ zeera, garam masala*. (I've provided English names in parentheses, though many of these may be just as unfamiliar to the reader as the Indian names.)

Some dishes are so well known by their Indian names that it is almost impossible to substitute a translation—

biryani, korma, lassi, masala, naan, pullao, raita, roti, tik-ka—to name a few. And who doesn't know *chai?* If you haven't heard these words already, you will figure them out quickly enough with the help of the **glossary**. If the glossary and my annotations do not help, you can always check the web. The Internet and commercially produced cookbooks offer a rich range of resources.

Of Pots and Pans and Other Utensils

Be assured, you can manage Indian cooking with your normal kitchen utensils, but heavy-bottomed pans are particularly helpful for frying spices on high heat and then braising. You might want to add a few other items to your kitchen shelf, but do not feel that you must re-stock. The following list is truly advisory.

A **karhai** (also transliterated **kadhai**) is an Indian version of a wok (with rounded base and handles) and is really excellent for all levels of frying. Indian-style vegetables are frequently cooked in a karhai.

Two items that do qualify as essential are a **spice grinder** and a regular **blender** or **food processor**. Since ground spices lose their flavor over time, it is better to buy small packets of ground spices or better still to grind small quantities of whole spices yourself. (If grinding at home, use a coffee grinder "dedicated" to spices.) A **mortar and pestle** can also grind or coarsely crush spices but are labor intensive if you want to grind finely. Additionally, you will need the blender or food processor to make spice pastes (combining dry ground spices with onion, ginger, garlic, and the like).

You will find frequent references to **pressure cookers** in the recipes. These devices are frequently used to cut down on cooking time (especially when several elaborate dishes are being prepared), but, again, they are not essential. Certainly, Indian cuisine evolved to sophisticated levels long before pressure cookers were invented.

A **tava** (also **tawa**) is a small, heavy, slightly concave, iron griddle, good for cooking chapatis and other Indian breads (see recipes in this volume). A regular cast-iron griddle works just as well.

Other handy utensils, again, convenient but not necessary, are **thalis** and **katoris**. Thalis are round, metal platters with a fairly high rim. Though used traditionally for serving a meal (in place of a dinner plate), they are also handy in the kitchen for stacking chopped vegetables or other cut foods. Katoris are small bowls, typically placed on a thali for "soupy" dishes, but they can also come in handy when you are preparing a meal: you can measure out your spices in small quantities in katoris. These containers are usually made of stainless steel.

Spices

Spices have been integral to Indian cooking for thousands of years and have played a vital role in shaping India's history since earliest times. Western traders and explorers sailed the high seas, lured by the fabled "spice of the Indies." Christopher Columbus, as Heather Whipp tells us in "How the Spice Trade Changed the World," was "searching for a quicker route to India [and spices], when he bumped into the Americas instead" (*LiveScience*). The spice trade, like the silk trade, was one of the forces that ushered in "The Age of Discovery" in the West and ultimately powered the engine of empire, resulting in a shift from trade to colonial dominance.

Countless are the uses of spices. They add variety and interest to many foods and satisfy the palate. But aside from that, they are useful as preservatives in warm climates. They are also associated with several health benefits, many of which have been scientifically proven. If you explore the web, you will find various home remedies using Indian spices. Some of these benefits are mentioned in the glossary.

It's a good idea to stock your spice shelf with a few basic spices. Some recipes call for whole spices, which keep for years. When used, they are traditionally left in the food when it is served, continuing to add flavor long after it is cooked. (Cloves and cardamom are good examples of long-lasting flavors that keep even when you freeze foods.) If you prefer, however, you may remove the spices before serving or freezing. Other recipes require ground spices, which you can buy in packets from Indian and international food and grocery stores.

Garam masala is one of the most popular of these. Being very fragrant, it is typically added at the end of the cooking phase and used sparingly. As mentioned earlier, if you like, grind spices in small quantities and store. Like coffee—there is nothing better than fresh ground!

You will, with experience, decide which spices you favor. Keep in mind that "spicy" does not necessarily mean "hot." Spicy food is fragrant, or pungent, or sharp. It can also be subtle. And it may or may not be "fired up" with chilli peppers. Some dishes may emphasize a particular scent (say, cardamom) that will dominate. Several highly aromatic spices will intensify after cooking, so it is best to start with small quantities. Discover what works for you and for those you plan to share your meals with.

Often, people unfamiliar with Indian food automatically think "curry" when you mention Indian food, frequently mistaking curry for a spice. Curry is in fact a category of prepared food (in consistency rather like a stew, with plentiful gravy or sauce). It is certainly not a spice, though you can buy curry powders that are combinations of spices used in curries.

Eating Styles

Diversity affects even eating styles in India. The traditional way food is served varies with geographic region; whether you are urban or rural; your particular ethnic/religious background; and many other considerations. Commonly, a meal is served on a *thali* with *katoris* (see p. 12), where rice, breads, and non-liquid vegetables (referred to as "dry") are separated from soupy dishes. South Indians have a wonderful, ecologically wise tradition—food is served on a freshly washed banana leaf. No styrofoam, no plastic. And few dishes to wash! In urban areas, western-style crockery and silverware are used, particularly in restaurants, and increasingly in private homes.

Water is served with the meal or right after. In a warm country with a spicy cuisine, this is a very practical option. Beverages, alcoholic or otherwise, are typically not served with your meal. If you are in a westernized household or living in the West, and if your host does serve alcoholic drinks, you will be offered these before dinner. And coffee and tea are not served after a meal. They make their appearance with breakfast, at mid-morning break or afternoon tea-time, or when guests drop in.

Traditionally, food is eaten with the right hand only, without silverware. You are expected to wash your hands before and after. (And for the very posh, even a "finger bowl" may be brought to the table after a meal so guests can rinse their fingers.) Breads are broken by hand and used to scoop up the food. The rice is mixed with the soupy foods. Here, as with all things Indian, there is much diversity, and many homes in urban areas provide some silverware with a meal.

Garnishes

Typically, fresh cilantro is used to brighten the look of dals and cooked vegetables. Often in Indian foods, vegetables are cooked long to enhance the flavors of the spices. A sprinkling of fresh cilantro balances the resulting loss of bright color. Cilantro does have a strong and distinctive flavor, so use according to your taste.

Thin onion rings and wedges of lemon are often served with kababs or along with other fresh vegetables.

Chopped almonds and pistachios, and, of course, edible silver leaf **(see glossary)** are popular as toppings for pullaos, sweets, and desserts.

You can, however, be as creative as you wish with your garnishes.

Hospitality

Indian hospitality is legendary and has a long tradition. In his well-researched account, *Indian Food: A Historical Companion*, K. T. Achaya recounts Hindu practices of hospitality as recorded in Vedic texts hundreds of years before the Common Era. Composed in Sanskrit, these ancient and sacred texts emphasize the honored position that guests have in a household and even specify the foods to be offered to visitors, including an "ambrosial" beverage, *madhuparka.*

The tradition of warmly welcoming a guest continues even today in our immigrant communities. Visitors, even those who drop by casually, are always offered some form of food and drink. And when you eat in an Indian home, you will be pressed many times to have yet one more helping. Hospitality becomes not only a sacred duty but a means of celebration.

A Nutritionist's View of Indian Cuisine

Vijaya Jain, Nutrition Consultant

The art and science of Indian cooking have evolved significantly over India's long history, mirroring various food traditions brought into the country by conquerors, invaders, traders, and travelers. However, despite the many contacts with other cultures, Indian cuisine has not lost its original identity; rather, it has grown richer with the assimilation of myriad influences. This is very apparent in India's unique regional cuisines, where each region's food specialties reflect both local culture and geographical location.

The origins of Indian food traditions have been traced back 5,000 years, when the normal diet consisted of fruit, vegetables, meat, grain, dairy products, and honey. Although India was not originally a vegetarian culture, a substantial and highly balanced vegetarian cuisine evolved early, influenced by Hinduism's growing respect for the principle of nonviolence (*ahimsa*) and by early religions such as Buddhism and Jainism, both of which originated in India (6th century BCE) and both of which emphasized the sanctity of all life.

Ancient Sanskrit texts from the Vedic period (1500 BCE) indicate that India had developed a sophisticated food-classification schema integral to a medical system called Ayurveda, which exists even today. This complex and nutritional system categorized foods by their impact on the body and mind and in particular emphasized nonmeat diets. Gradually, vegetarianism became widespread, and beef eating came to be avoided among many groups of people. Although by no means exclusively vegetarian today, Indian cuisine certainly affirms that a vegetarian diet is a powerful and pleasurable way to achieve good health.

The vegetarian eating pattern is based on a wide variety of foods that are satisfying, delicious, and healthful.

The position statement issued by the American Dietetic Association states that "appropriately planned vegetarian diets including total vegetarian or vegan diets are healthful, nutritionally adequate, and may provide health benefits in the treatment of diseases" ("Vegetarian Diets" in *Journal of the American Dietetic Association,* 2009). The staples of Indian cuisine are grains—mainly rice and wheat flour, which provide the bulk of calories and a variety of pulses, legumes, or dals that are the main sources of protein. All essential amino acids necessary for humans are present only in animal products and in soybeans. All other plant proteins are incomplete as they lack one or more of the essential amino acids. However, cereal-legume based combination dishes offer complementary sources of protein, thus meeting the need for all the essential amino acids. Milk and milk products, namely yogurt and paneer (homemade unripened cheese) also supply complete proteins. Additionally, a wide variety of fruits, vegetables, nuts, and spices provide an array of micronutrients, phytochemicals, and antioxidants and thus contribute to making a balanced Indian meal.

Indian foods are characterized by their aromatic spices, which often help to preserve foods. Whole or dry, powdered spices and combinations of spices known as *masalas* provide the unique flavors and taste to Indian dishes (B. Narula and L. I. Tettoni, *The Food of India: Authentic Recipes from the Spicy Subcontinent*, Periplus, 2000). Several fresh or dried herbs (often leaves) such as bay leaf and the leaves of coriander, fenugreek, and mint are commonly used to add their distinctive flavors to Indian cuisine. But as anyone who cooks in India will tell you, spices are combined individually in each kitchen. Each region has its specialties, and each chef creates his or her distinctive blend.

Not only are these natural spices and herbs pleasing to the palate, but according to traditional medical beliefs, they are beneficial to the body as well. Many of them are said to have what Ayurvedic medicine designates as a heating or cooling and calming effect on the body. Recent research indicates that certain spices aid in the digestive processes and provide antiseptic and anti-inflammatory properties (K. Patel and K. Srinivasan, "Digestive stimulant action of spices: a myth or reality?" in *Indian Journal of Medical Research*, 2004.) India's cuisine may be built on traditional theories and practices that go back millennia, but like all things Indian, it continues to grow and survive by adapting to current conditions. For those in search of a vegetarian diet, Indian cuisine is designed to balance health and wellness and thus offers a diet that is complete, appropriate, and satisfying.

Some Practical Tips

To get you started, here are some hints and a few basic recipes for prepared ingredients.

Read the Section Introductions
Though brief, these introductions provide some background about the category of foods in that section.

Use the Glossary
Almost every recipe contains ingredients or terms that need explanation. Those that appear only occasionally are flagged with a *See glossary reminder. Others recur often enough that you will soon get to know them (for example, ghee, which is clarified butter). These words are mostly translated in text, but for a fuller explanation consult the glossary. (Web sources are also helpful.) Some words simply resist translation (for example, dal). The glossary or the introduction to the relevant section offers an explanation or comment.

Too Many Spices?
Don't be dismayed by the long lists of ingredients. Many are used in small quantities—a pinch, a dash, a half-teaspoon. You will soon recognize certain clusters and combinations, such as (a) onion, ginger, garlic; (b) ground cumin, ground coriander, turmeric, hing; (c) cumin seeds, mustard seeds; (d) whole cinnamon, cardamom, clove.

It helps to set out the spices before getting started. Experienced cooks often keep a platter next to the stove with little bowls containing different ground spices.

Prepared Ingredients
Some items need to be prepared ahead of time. Most can be bought readymade, but if you want to make your own, here are some simple directions.

Garam Masala

Garam masalas are blends of ground spices, and the combination varies with each individual cook. This recipe comes from Shuchi Agrawal.

1 tablespoon green cardamom seeds
1 tablespoon black cardamom seeds
1 tablespoon cloves
1 tablespoon black peppercorns
½ nutmeg, in pieces
8–10 bay leaves
1 tablespoon stick cinnamon, in pieces
1 tablespoon cumin seeds
1 tablespoon mace
2 teaspoons black cumin seeds*
*See glossary

In a heavy pan or griddle on medium heat, dry roast all the ingredients for 2 to 4 minutes. Cool and mix the spices. Grind coarse or fine, according to your preference. Store in a bottle with a tight cap. The mixture will keep its fragrance for several months.

Dry-Roasted Cumin

Heat a heavy pan on medium heat and add 3 tablespoons of whole cumin. Stir frequently or shake the pan to prevent burning. When the seeds darken and release their aroma, remove and spread on a plate to cool. Grind with a mortar and pestle or in a spice grinder. Store in a bottle with a tight cap. Roasted cumin has a very different aroma from regular cumin. Use sparingly. Good as a garnish on raitas.

Paneer (homemade unripened Indian cheese)

Paneer is an important source of protein in vegetarian diets. It is available at Indian or international food and grocery stores, usually as a block or in cubes. (Avoid frozen paneer, which loses texture and flavor.) Here are some helpful hints from Indra Aggarwal.

Paneer can be cubed, sliced, or crumbled, depending on the dish you are preparing. When cubed, it can be used in pakoras, marinated and broiled like tikkas, or cooked with vegetables. It can also be incorporated into various desserts. You can deep-fry or pan-fry it, bake it, or even use it in in lasagna. The ways you make your paneer will differ slightly, depending on how you plan to use it.

Paneer Recipe
Ingredients: ½ gallon milk (whole or 2%); 2 ounces fresh or bottled lemon juice.

In a saucepan, bring the milk to a boil and add the lemon juice while the milk is boiling. Remove the pot from the stove. The lemon juice causes the milk to curdle and separate from the liquid (whey). Add more lemon juice if needed to curdle the milk.

Once the whey has drained, pour the solids through a strainer and squeeze out the remaining liquid by pressing down with a big spoon. The paneer will be crumbly. For sweets, such as Rasgulla (p. 282), mash the paneer immediately until smooth.

For other sweets, for example, Almond Fudge (p. 280), put the solids in a muslin cloth and hang the cloth to drain for a couple of hours. Then coarsely crumble.

To make the paneer firm in order to cube it, compress the solids and place under a heavy weight (like a pot of water) for 2 to 3 hours till compacted.

_____

Tamarind Extract
Dried tamarind is available from Indian and international food stores. Soak a lump of tamarind for at least 2 hours (longer if possible) in ½ cup of warm water. Over a bowl, remove the seeds, and work the tamarind with your fingers to break it down to a pulp. Add two cups of water to the pulp and press through a strainer into a bowl. Dis-

card the stringy part, keeping as much of the thick liquid as possible.

The Power of Yogurt

Unflavored yogurt is an integral part of Indian cuisine. It is used in curries, marinades, raitas; in savory and sweet dishes; just plain or with sugar. Yogurt contains digestive enzymes and "friendly" bacteria that calm the stomach and promote intestinal health. Additionally, it is more easily tolerated by the lactose intolerant. In South India, plain yogurt is served with plain rice at the end of a meal—a wise way to conclude an often fiery repast.

Most Indian homes make their yogurt daily, which is more textured and rather different in flavor from American yogurt. Store-bought yogurt in the United States is different but adequate.

Let's Lighten Up

Like all tasty foods, Indian cooking often uses ingredients high in calories and fats. The challenge is to enjoy this cuisine but to keep the calories in check. Here are some suggestions:

- **Reduce deep frying.** For example, if a recipe calls for fried onions, use half the amount. With paneer, omit frying it before use. Try substituting tofu; let your spices help you forget that tofu is not paneer.
- When frying, cook on **lower heat with less oil**. This process may take longer but will still retain the flavor.
- **Reduce the coconut.** Even though delicious, coconut is high in saturated fat. Use smaller quantities. When **coconut milk** is used to thicken gravy, reduce the quantity and add rice powder. Use "lite" coconut milk.
- **Replace or reduce the ghee (clarified butter).** Substitute olive or canola oil. (Add a little ghee just to capture the flavor.)
- **Select low-fat or fat-free milk** products. Evaporated unsweetened skim milk can help thicken a milk dessert.

- **Limit the meats**—discover and enjoy a balanced vegetarian diet.
- Always **trim the fat and skins** off meats.
- **Reduce sodium**. There are plenty of spices to make up for salt.
- **Lightly pre-cook** the vegetables and then further cook for less time and with less oil.
- **Replace frying** vegetables with roasting and grilling.
- **Discover the magic of tarka.**

Tarka

This method of seasoning is widely used and goes by many names **(see glossary).** Tarkas can be very rich but they can also be simple and relatively low in oil. The process described here is necessarily general because tarkas vary with the food being seasoned. (Check individual recipes in this collection. Tarkas may be called by that name or referred to as seasoning.)

Tarkas season foods that are pre-cooked (dals), or lightly cooked (some vegetables), or sometimes even uncooked (raitas). Heat the oil in a small pan and add specified whole spices, such as mustard seeds, cumin seeds, hing, whole dried chillies, sliced garlic. Stir-fry rapidly, and add the hot oil to the dal, vegetable, or raita. Braise as needed. (Braising will not apply to raitas.)

Tinker, Tailor

And finally, remember you are embarking on an adventure. Try the recipes and tinker with them. Tailor them to your own preferences. Experiment on the way and enjoy your journey!

You are what you eat.

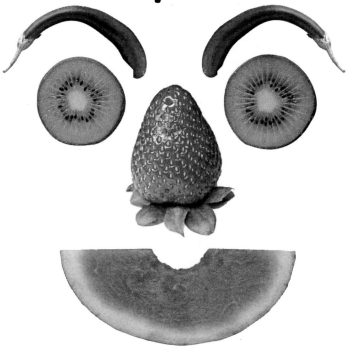

For flavorful and healthy eating for breakfast, lunch and dinner, visit Strawberry Fields, our area's premier natural foods store.

Strawberry Fields

306 W. SPRINGFIELD AVENUE, URBANA • 328-1655
WWW.STRAWBERRY-FIELDS.COM

❦

Appetizers & Snacks

Typically in India, there is no custom of serving appetizers before a meal. In fact, there is no main course, and most dishes are served at the same time. Residing in the West, Indians have become accustomed to serving appetizers, a few of which appear in this section (and not all of which are distinctively Indian). Many appetizers are considered snack foods in India. And if there is one thing Indians love par excellence, it is snack food—crunchy, spicy, served up with or without chutney. These foods may be sold by vendors on street corners or in *chaat* shops that cater to just snacks and sweets. Snacks make their appearance at tea-time, at parties, or at morning break, fresh cooked or pre-packaged. There is nothing like a snack to instantly satisfy the jaded palate. Several are readily available at local Indian and international food stores.

Roasted Sweet Peppers with Feta Cheese

Jaya Kumar

Serves 6

24 small sweet peppers (mixed colors)
3 tablespoons olive oil
16 ounces crumbled feta cheese
Crushed red pepper to taste
Chopped cilantro (6–12 leaves)
2 teaspoons chopped fresh oregano
Salt and pepper
Garnish: Crushed pecans or toasted pine nuts

Heat oven to 350 degrees F.

Split open (but do not separate) the peppers, and remove the seeds and white fiber. Mix together the olive oil, feta cheese, red pepper, cilantro, oregano, salt, and pepper.

Fill the peppers with the stuffing and lay carefully on a cookie sheet. Brush with a little olive oil and bake for 5 to 10 minutes.

Arrange on a platter and sprinkle with chopped pecans or toasted pine nuts.

Roasted Eggplant & Red Bell Pepper Spread

Anita Goodnight

Serves 4–6

1 eggplant cut into 1-inch pieces (peel a little of the skin off before cutting)

1 red bell pepper cut into 1-inch pieces

1 medium red onion, cut into 1-inch pieces

2–3 cloves garlic, chopped

2 tablespoons olive oil

1 teaspoon coarse salt

½ teaspoon black pepper

¼ teaspoon ground cumin

¼ teaspoon garam masala

Crushed red pepper (to taste)

3–4 tablespoons fresh lemon juice

1 tablespoon cilantro, chopped

Preheat oven to 400 degrees F.

Toss the eggplant pieces, bell pepper, onion, and garlic with 2 tablespoons of olive oil, salt, and black pepper. Layer the mixed pieces on a baking sheet. Bake for 30 minutes.

Place roasted vegetables in a food processer. Pulse 2 to 3 times. Add the ground cumin, garam masala, crushed red pepper, lemon juice, and chopped cilantro. Pulse again 2 to 3 times to make a textured paste.

Add more lemon juice as needed.

Serve with crackers or pita bread.

Cheese Straws

Indra Aggarwal

Editor's note: This makes a good tea-time snack.

Serves 8–10

1 cup grated cheese
   sharp Colby
3 cups all-purpose flour
2 tablespoons semolina
½ teaspoon ajwain*
   (carom seeds)

¼ teaspoon salt
¼ cup of water or more
   as needed
3 ounces oil for deep
   frying

*See glossary

Mix all the ingredients well. Add enough water to form a dough and knead well. The dough should be hard. The texture of the dough will be better if left for about 30 minutes before rolling.

Roll thin and cut into narrow strips. Deep fry on medium-to-low heat until brown.

Fried Matzoh

(Matzoh Brei)

P. R. Balgopal

Contributor's note: A traditional Passover breakfast done Indian style —"Hinju" Matzoh!

Serves 3–4

3 eggs
Salt and pepper to taste
3 sheets of matzoh
2 tablespoons butter or
   margarine
1 medium onion, diced
   small

½ cup green bell pepper,
   diced
½ cup fresh mushrooms,
   diced
½ cut green chilli
Garnish: Chopped fresh
   cilantro

Beat the eggs and add salt and pepper. Set aside.

Run the matzoh sheets under warm water and break them into small pieces. Add the matzoh pieces to the beaten eggs.

Melt the butter or margarine over medium heat in a pan. Sauté the onion, bell pepper, and mushrooms. After the vegetables have browned, add the matzohs and eggs and cook on low heat. Add the green chilli. You can either cook the eggs and other ingredients as an omelette or as scrambled eggs.

Top with chopped cilantro before serving.

Savory Pastries with Potato Filling
(Samosa)

Shuchi Agrawal

Editor's note: Over the last few years, samosas have become immensely popular in the United States as a party food. Although available in the freezer section of any international or Indian grocery store, fresh homemade samosas are unbeatable. They are always served with one or two chutneys and go well with pre-dinner drinks. Adapted and reprinted with permission from www.chezshuchi.com.

Makes 16 samosas

For the pastry shell & flour paste

1½ cups refined flour
3 tablespoons melted ghee (clarified butter) or hot oil
¼ teaspoon salt

½ teaspoon ajwain (carom seeds)*

*See glossary

For the filling

2 tablespoons oil for frying the stuffing
1 teaspoon cumin seeds
1½ inch piece of fresh ginger, peeled and finely chopped
2 green chillies, sliced into rounds
10–12 cashew nuts, chopped into quarters
1 teaspoon garam masala

½ teaspoon red chilli powder
2 teaspoons ground coriander
1 teaspoon amchur (dried mango powder)
8 medium potatoes, boiled and mashed
1 cup peas
Salt to taste
2 tablespoons fresh cilantro, chopped

1 cup oil for deep frying (or more as needed)

The pastry shell
First make the flour paste: Take 1 teaspoon flour and 4 teaspoons of water and mix well. Set aside till you are making the samosas.

Mix together the flour, hot oil (or ghee), salt, and ajwain. Add a little water and knead the dough into a smooth, stiff mixture. Cover and set aside for about 30 minutes.

The filling
In a karhai (or wok), heat the oil on medium heat. Add the cumin seeds when hot. When the seeds sizzle and start to brown, add the ginger and green chillies and fry for a few seconds. Add the cashews and fry for half a minute. Add the remaining spices except the salt.

Add the mashed potatoes and green peas and mix well. Add the salt to taste. Fry on low for 10 to 15 minutes. Mix in the chopped cilantro. Set aside.

Making the samosas
Divide the dough into 8 round portions. Roll each ball to make a not-too-thin disc. Cut the disc into 2 halves.

Dip your index finger into the flour paste and apply to the straight edge of the semicircle. Pick up the half disc and fold the straight edge, bringing together the dampened edges so they are sealed. You should now have a small triangular pocket, like a cone.

Fill the cone with the potato mixture, and seal the rounded edges, after moistening your fingertips with the paste. Repeat the process with the rest of the portions.

In the karhai (or wok), heat 1 cup oil and deep fry the samosas on medium-low, until golden brown. (This takes about 30 minutes per batch.) Place on a paper towel to drain.

Serve hot with a choice of coriander, mint, and tamarind chutneys. (See chutney recipes in *Chutneys & Pickles*.)

Vegetable Fritters
(Pakora)

Annie Pawar

Editor's note: Pakoras are a popular tea-time snack. Like tempura, they are dipped in batter and deep fried. Pakoras taste best served immediately, when they are hot and crisp.

Serves 4

1 cup gram flour (besan)
¼ cup water
1 tablespoon green chillies (finely chopped)
½ teaspoon red chilli powder
½ teaspoon coarsely ground cumin seeds
½ teaspoon garam masala
Pinch of turmeric
Salt to taste
¾ cup oil for deep frying
2 cups of chopped vegetables (thin-sliced blanched potato, fine rings of onion, small spinach leaves, blanched cauliflower florets, other vegetables of choice*)

*Paneer is also an option. See p. 20.

Mix the besan and water and add all the spices to make a thick batter that can coat the vegetables.

Heat the oil in a frying pan on medium-high till very hot but not smoking.

Dip each piece of vegetable in the batter and deep fry 6 to 8 pieces at a time until golden brown.

Place fritters on a paper towel to drain. Serve immediately with a couple of chutneys. (Mint, coriander, and tamarind are popular choices. See recipes in *Chutneys & Pickles*.)

Savory Snack

Rashmi Kapoor

Serves 6–8

3 cups Corn Chex cereal
3 cups Rice Chex cereal
3 cups Rice Crispies cereal
1 cup roasted peanuts
½ cup roasted cashews
½ cup raisins
Salt to taste
1 tablespoon red chilli powder
2 tablespoons chaat masala* (any brand will do)

2 tablespoons canola or other vegetable oil
1 tablespoon mustard seeds
1 tablespoon cumin seeds
A handful of fresh curry leaves (optional)
2–3 chopped green chillies, seeds removed (optional)

*Available at Indian and international food and grocery stores. **See glossary.**

Mix the cereals, nuts, and raisins in a large container. Add salt, red chilli powder, and chaat masala, and mix well.

Heat the oil in a small pan. Add the mustard and cumin seeds. When the mustard seeds pop, remove from the heat and add the curry leaves and green chilli (if using). Pour this into the cereal and stir gently to combine.

Store in an airtight container and serve as a snack.

Spicy Garbanzos
(Sundal)

Deepa Madhubalan

Contributor's note: The name of this snack is pronounced *soon-dull.*

Serves 4

- 1 20-ounce can garbanzo beans
- 1 teaspoon oil
- ¾ teaspoon mustard seeds
- 1 teaspoon cumin seeds
- 1 medium onion chopped fine
- 2–3 serrano green chillies (jalapeños if you want the dish hotter)
- ½ teaspoon turmeric
- ½–1 teaspoons salt
- 1–2 tablespoons grated fresh or dry coconut (optional)
- ½ cup water
- 1–2 teaspoons lime/lemon juice
- *Garnish:* 2–3 teaspoons chopped fresh cilantro

Drain and rinse the garbanzo beans and set aside.

Heat the oil in a saucepan on medium heat. When hot, add the mustard seeds and then the cumin seeds. After the seeds brown a little, add the chopped onions and the green chillies. Cook for a few minutes until the onions turn transparent.

Add the turmeric and salt and then the drained beans. Mix everything thoroughly and add ½ cup of water. Add the grated coconut, if using. Cover the pan and cook on low heat for about 10 minutes.

Add lime juice before serving. Garnish with the chopped cilantro. Serve hot.

Vegetable Kababs on Skewers
(Noorani Seekh Kabab)

Anupam Agrawal

Contributor's note: Lucknow, once the capital of a princely state called Awadh, is famous for its wide variety of kababs **(see glossary)**. Though kababs are traditionally made with meat, this recipe offers a low-fat, easy-to-make vegetarian option.

Makes 14–16 kababs

½ cup chana dal

1½ teaspoons salt or to taste

1⅓ cup water

2 cups mashed or crumbled paneer‡

2 tablespoons bell peppers, finely chopped

¼ cup cabbage, finely chopped (optional)

2–3 tablespoons carrots, finely chopped

1 medium onion, finely chopped

2 green chillies, finely chopped

2 teaspoons grated fresh ginger

¼ teaspoon red chilli powder

½ teaspoon garam masala

½ teaspoon chaat masala*

1 teaspoon tandoori masala*

2 teaspoons melted ghee (clarified butter)

*Available at Indian and international food and grocery stores. **See glossary,** under **Dals.**

‡**See p. 20**

Wash and soak the chana dal for half an hour. Boil the dal with ½ teaspoon salt in 1⅓ cups water until tender (the dal should not be soupy). If the dal is too liquid, cook further until it thickens. Let it cool and then mash (this can be done in a mixer or blender).

In a mixing bowl, combine the mashed dal with the crumbled/mashed paneer, chopped bell pepper, cabbage (if using), carrot, onion, green chillies, and ginger.

Add the spices—red chilli powder, garam masala, chaat masala, and tandoori masala and mix thoroughly. Make about 16 oval-shaped kababs (rolls). Hold each kabab in your hand and gently slide a skewer through the center. Press and shape the kabab into an oval (rather like a sausage).

Brush a little ghee on every side of the kabab.

Cooking Options

Barbecue
The most traditional way to prepare the kababs is to grill them over charcoal.

In the oven
Preheat oven to 350 F. Spread butter paper or foil on a cookie tray and arrange all the skewers on the tray. Bake till the kababs are golden brown. This takes about 20 to 25 minutes.

On a gas stove
Put a wire mesh over a medium flame, hold the skewers one at a time over the flame, and cook till the kababs are brown.

Deep frying
The kababs can also be deep fried. Shape the kababs into ovals, but do not skewer them. In a wok, heat 1½ cups oil on medium high and fry the kababs till they are golden brown.

Serving suggestion: This appetizer goes best with coriander-mint chutney (see recipe in *Chutneys & Pickles*).

Savory Semolina
(Upama)

Yamuna Kachru

Contributor's note: This is a South Indian dish, popular both as a snack and breakfast food. Total preparation time (if no chopping of onions and vegetables is involved): 30 minutes. To save time, you can substitute 1 cup of frozen mixed vegetables that have green beans, carrots, peas and corn.

Serves 4

1 cup quick-cooking semolina

2 tablespoons vegetable oil

1 teaspoon mustard seeds

½ teaspoon cumin seeds

1 teaspoon urad dal

1 teaspoon chana dal

1 inch fresh ginger, chopped fine or grated

2 hot green chillies, slit lengthwise (seeds removed)

A few curry leaves

1 medium onion, finely chopped (optional)

1 medium potato, chopped into ¼-inch cubes

1 carrot, chopped into ¼-inch pieces

¼ cup green peas frozen or fresh

3 cups of water

½ teaspoon salt (or to taste)

1 tablespoon butter

2–3 tablespoons lemon juice to taste

⅔ cups dry-roasted cashew nuts (or peanuts)*

Finely chopped cilantro leaves

*I prefer cashew nuts for their flavor.

Roast the semolina on medium heat in a thick-bottomed pan till it turns pinkish in color (not brown). Set aside.

In a two-quart, heavy-bottomed pan, heat the oil on medium heat; add the mustard and cumin seeds and fry till they pop; add the urad and chana dal and fry till they turn light brown.

Add the ginger, green chillies, and curry leaves and sauté for 6 to 7 seconds. Add the onions, if using, and fry till they turn golden brown. Add the chopped (or frozen vegetables) and sauté for two minutes. Add 3 cups of water and bring the mixture to a boil.

Cook the vegetables for 5 to 6 minutes till the potato and carrot pieces are tender. Add the salt and stir. Lower the heat.

Add the semolina slowly, constantly stirring. (As the mixture starts to thicken, it may sputter, so watch out so as to avoid getting splattered!) Keep stirring till the mixture turns to a crumbly consistency. Add the butter for flavor and stir to combine.

Turn the heat off. Add the lemon juice and mix well. Sprinkle the cashew nuts and chopped cilantro on top.

Serve hot with your favorite chutney.

South Indian Spicy Noodles

Vijaya Jain

Contributor's note: This dish is commonly served at breakfast or as a snack.

Serves 3–4

8 ounces rice or wheat noodles (packaged)
2 tablespoons oil
½ teaspoon mustard seeds
½ teaspoon cumin seeds
½ teaspoon urad dal
2 tablespoons onions, chopped
1 teaspoon fresh ginger, finely chopped
2 fresh curry leaves, chopped
1 tablespoon dry un-sweetened coconut flakes or freshly shredded coconut
Salt to taste
Garnish: 1 tablespoon chopped fresh cilantro

Cook the noodles according to the package directions. Drain the noodles and rinse in cold water. Set aside to cool.

In a medium-size saucepan, heat the cooking oil over medium heat. Add the mustard and cumin seeds. When they start to sputter, add the urad dal and fry till it turns a light brown.

Add the onions and fry lightly until light brown; add the chopped ginger. Fry for 2 to 3 minutes.

Add the curry leaves, coconut flakes, and the noodles. Mix well. Add salt to taste and remove from the heat.

Garnish with cilantro.

∞

Fish & Seafood

Vegetarians define themselves in different ways. Some will eat fish and seafood but not the flesh of other animals. As in all countries, the kind of fish available in India is determined by region. Coastal regions offer seafood and fish; prior to refrigeration and freezing, landlocked areas and interior regions focused on river and lake fish. Dried and salted fish is also an option for those growing up far from the coast.

Bengal and Kerala in particular are famous for their fish dishes. Some Bengalis refer to fish as "Ganga Phal" or fruit of the Ganga, the sacred river of India known to the West as the Ganges. Indians enjoy their stereotypes of each region and often view Bengalis as highly intelligent. The reason for this brilliance, we were told as children, was that Bengalis ate a lot of fish, and this diet replenished their brain cells, turning them into poets, writers, artists, and thinkers!

Bengali Yogurt-Fish Curry

Krishna Bhowmik

Serves 4

1 pound buffalo fish (or halibut) with bones or without bones

2 large onions for the paste & 1 medium onion chopped

2-inch piece of fresh ginger, peeled

½ teaspoon of turmeric

Curry powder to taste

1 cup plain yogurt

2 tablespoons canola oil

1 tablespoon chopped fresh garlic

5 whole cloves

5 green cardamoms pods

2 3-inch long cinnamon sticks (whole)

Sugar to taste

One or two small hot chilli peppers (optional), chopped

Salt to taste

Cut the fish into pieces, each approximately 2 x 1 inches. In a food processor, grind the two large onions with the ginger. Mix the onion and ginger paste, turmeric, and curry powder with the yogurt. Cover the fish with this mixture.

In a separate pan, heat 2 tablespoons of canola oil over medium heat; add the chopped onion and lightly brown the mixture. Add the garlic, whole cloves, cardamom pods, cinnamon sticks, and sugar. When the mixture becomes aromatic, add the fish and yogurt mixture. If using chilli peppers, add them at this time. Add the salt. Cover the pan fairly tight and simmer for 6 to 7 minutes.

Serving suggestion: Fish curry goes best with plain white rice.

Blackened Spicy Salmon

P. R. Balgopal

Adapted from *Indique Chefs.*

Serves 4–6

4 salmon fillets, 4 to 6 ounces each, preferably wild salmon

4 teaspoons ginger and garlic paste

4 teaspoons fresh lemon juice

4 teaspoons olive oil for the rub + 2 teaspoons for the skillet

Salt to taste

8 whole cloves

3 teaspoons coriander seeds

½ teaspoon red pepper flakes

1 teaspoon cumin seeds

1 teaspoon whole black peppercorns

1 teaspoon tandoori masala or karhai masala (packaged spices)*

8 lemon slices

Garnish: ½ cup chopped fresh cilantro

*These are powdered spice mixes found in any Indian or international grocery.

Preheat oven to 350 degrees F.

With wild salmon, leave the skin on (since it is thin). If using farm-raised salmon, remove the skin. Pat fillets dry.

Mix the ginger and garlic paste with lemon juice, olive oil, and salt. Rub this on the salmon fillets on both sides. Press 2 cloves onto each fillet. Marinate for 30 minutes.

In a heavy skillet over medium heat, toast the coriander seeds, red pepper flakes, cumin seeds, and peppercorns. After a few minutes, when the spices become fragrant, remove from the heat and let them cool. Coarsely grind the toasted spices in a spice grinder and mix with the tandoori masala or karhai masala. Generously apply the spices to the skin-free side of each fillet.

In an ovenproof skillet, heat 2 teaspoons olive oil on high and place the fillets with the skin-free (masala) side facing down so they can blacken. Sear for just ONE minute—or till the spices form a visible crust, and then flip the fillets over gently. Cook for 30 seconds, skin side down, and remove from the stove top.

Place the skillet in a preheated oven. Put the lemon slices on top of the fillet and bake fillets, skin-free (masala) side facing up for about 10 minutes or till the salmon is cooked. *Do not overcook.*

Serve with rice pilaf and a cooked green vegetable, lightly spiced—cabbage and peas, or fresh green beans and a green salad.

Grill Option
After blackening the salmon in the skillet, place the fillets on a very hot grill, with the skin side down (masala side facing up). Grill for 5 minutes.

Shallow-Fried Fish

Manisha Bhagwat

Contributor's note: This is so tasty that your family will finish it even before the meal starts!

Serves 4

1 pound any firm-fleshed fish*
2 teaspoons oil
1½ teaspoons garlic paste
½ teaspoon ginger paste
½ teaspoon turmeric (plus ⅛ teaspoon for the rice coating)
2 teaspoons hot red chilli powder (plus ⅛ teaspoon for the rice coating)
¼ teaspoon ground black pepper
1 teaspoon tamarind pulp (or 2 tablespoons lemon juice in place of tamarind)
¾ teaspoon + ⅛ teaspoon salt
4 tablespoons rice flour
Oil for frying
Garnish: Chopped fresh cilantro and lemon wedges

*Halibut, haddock, catfish, mackerel, or pomfret from the Indian Ocean. Frozen pomfret is generally available at Asian groceries.

Wash and clean the fish. Cut the fish into 3-inch pieces, about ¼-inch thick. Pat dry with a paper towel. Rub 2 teaspoons of oil on the fish.

Mix together the garlic and ginger pastes with turmeric, red chilli powder, black pepper, tamarind pulp (or lemon juice) and ¾ teaspoon salt, and rub the fish gently with the mixture. Let stand for 15 to 20 minutes.

Mix the rice flour with ⅛ teaspoon each of turmeric, salt, and red chilli powder.

In a shallow skillet, add just enough oil to cover the bottom of the pan and heat on medium.

45

Lightly coat the fish pieces with the rice flour and arrange them in the hot oil. Let the fish pieces cook for 3 minutes and then turn them over very gently. Cook another 4 minutes, until the pieces are cooked through and crisp. Remove from the oil and place them on a paper towel to drain.

Arrange the fish on a serving platter with lemon wedges and sprinkle chopped fresh cilantro on the top.

Simply Fried Fish

Munni Rodrigues

Editor's note: Traditionally, this dish is made in Goa with a sea fish called *Bombil* (also known in English by the quaint name of *Bombay Duck*). It is possible, however, to substitute any white fish.

Serves 4

6 fillets of fish
1 tablespoon lemon juice
1 teaspoon red chilli powder (or to taste)
½ teaspoon turmeric
Salt to taste
Bread crumbs enough to coat the fish
2 tablespoons vegetable oil

Wash the fish and pat dry. Make a mixture of the lemon juice, red chilli powder, turmeric, and salt. Rub the mixture onto the fish on all sides. Coat the fish with bread crumbs.

In a heavy-bottomed pan, heat the oil on medium. When the oil begins to smoke, quickly fry the fish until it is cooked through and browned. Remove right away from the heat. Watch out for burning!

Serve with chapatis or rice and a vegetable.

Green Coconut Fish

Rajeshwari Pandharipande

Adapted and reprinted with permission from *The International Linguistic Gourmet Cookbook*, 1984, compiled and produced by the Department of Linguistics, University of Illinois at Urbana-Champaign.

Serves 4

1 pound catfish (cut into 3-inch pieces)
2 tablespoons dry, unsweetened coconut flakes
1 teaspoon cumin seeds
10 sprigs cilantro
½ teaspoon turmeric
7 large cloves of garlic
1 green jalapeño pepper
3 tablespoons lemon juice
1 tablespoon cooking oil
1 teaspoon salt

Wash and dry the pieces of fish and set aside.

Grind the coconut, cumin, cilantro, turmeric, garlic, and jalapeño together with the lemon juice to make a smooth paste. Use half the paste to marinate the fish for an hour. Set the other half aside.

Heat the oil on medium-low heat in a skillet for about 3 minutes. Add the reserved paste and fry for about 2 minutes. Add the fish and fry it for about 4 minutes.

Cover and cook for another 5 minutes or so.

Serve with rice or Indian bread.

Tuna Casserole
(Bal's Comfort Food Recipe)

P. R. Balgopal

Contributor's note: When your partner is an excellent cook, it is an arduous task to feed the kids when they are left in your care, as they not only miss their mother but her cooking too! So, your challenge is to cook simple yet tasty dishes.

Serves 4

1 can tuna (7– 8 ounces, in water or light oil)

8 ounces shell macaroni

4 tablespoons margarine

3 tablespoons finely chopped onion

3 tablespoons chopped green bell pepper

¼ cup chopped mushrooms

⅛ teaspoon each: black pepper, dry mustard, ginger powder

½ teaspoon cumin seeds, roasted and coarsely ground

¾ teaspoon seasoned salt

Pinch of curry powder (optional)

½ cup 2% milk

1 can cream of mushroom soup

½ cup frozen green peas, thawed (or broccoli florets, if you prefer)

1 cup shredded cheddar cheese (medium or mild)

1 can dry onion rings

Preheat oven to 350 degrees F.

Drain the tuna, and flake it with a fork.

Cook the macaroni in boiling water according to the package directions, drain, and set aside.

Melt the margarine in a large saucepan. Add chopped onion, bell pepper, and mushroom, and sauté over low heat for about 3 to 4 minutes till the onion becomes tender and golden brown.

Add the black pepper, dry mustard, ginger powder, dry-roasted ground cumin, salt, and curry powder (if using). Add milk and mushroom soup and stir over very low heat (this is the sauce).

Add drained macaroni, flaked tuna, and peas (or broccoli) to the sauce, and stir the mixture constantly for a few minutes.

Pour the mixture in a 2-quart buttered/greased casserole dish and bake for 25 minutes; then spread the cheese and onion rings on top and bake for another 10 to12 minutes or until the cheese is melted and the top is crisply brown.

Serving suggestions: Serve the casserole with salad and bread.

Variations: You can substitute cream of asparagus soup for mushroom soup and add fresh-cut asparagus to the mixture before baking.

Fenugreek-Flavored Grilled Tilapia

Zarina Hock

Serves 4

4 tilapia fillets
4 large cloves of garlic, crushed
2 tablespoons olive oil
½ teaspoon red pepper flakes
¼ teaspoon turmeric
½ teaspoon cayenne pepper
¼–½ teaspoon finely ground fenugreek seeds (this seed is flavorful but strong)
Juice of half a lemon (or more to taste)
2–3 teaspoons dry citrus dressing for fish (available at all groceries)
Salt to taste (remember, the citrus dressing is likely to be salted)

Place the tilapia in a dish and make a few slits in the fillets.

Crush the garlic cloves. In a cup or small bowl mix he garlic with the remaining ingredients except the fish to make a marinade. Pour the marinade onto the fillets and rub gently into both sides of each fillet. Allow the fish to marinate for at least an hour.

Lay the fillets on foil and place on the grill for twenty minutes until the fish is flaky. Tilapia cooks very quickly, so be careful not to overcook.

Hint: If using an oven, place the fish in an oven-proof dish and cook uncovered for 20 minutes at 400 degrees F.

Alternative: You can also use salmon. In that case, substitute dill weed for the citrus dressing. Grill or bake uncovered at 400 degrees F. for 20 minutes.

Kerala Fish Curry

Ania Loomba

Serves 4–6

For the dry masala

1 teaspoon peppercorns
2 tablespoons coriander
  seeds
¼ teaspoon fenugreek
  seeds
½ teaspoon fennel
1-inch stick
  cinnamon
6–7 dry curry leaves

Heat a skillet and roast all the spices for a few minutes
until fragrant. Grind together to make a powder.

For the fish curry

2½ pounds of firm fish,
  preferably steaks
3 tablespoons vegetable
  oil
2–3 red onions, chopped
  fine
4–5 cloves of garlic,
  crushed
1 teaspoon turmeric
Dry masala as prepared
  above
1 cup of water
1 tablespoon kokum,*
  soaked for 5 minutes
in water and cut to
  pencil thickness
1 teaspoon red chilli
  powder or 1 teaspoon
  cayenne pepper
½ teaspoon salt
4 green chillies, sliced
A few fresh curry leaves
1½ cups of coconut milk
  (available at Indian &
  international grocer-
  ies)

*Kokum is a tropical fruit that when dried serves as a souring
agent. If not available, use lime juice.

Wash and cut the fish into 3 to 4-inch pieces and set
aside.

Heat the oil over medium heat. Add the onions and fry till
they are translucent. Add the garlic and turmeric and fry.

Add the prepared dry masala mix. Immediately add 1 cup of water. Add the kokum, followed by the cayenne or red chilli powder and salt.

Add the fresh green chillies. Boil and simmer the sauce for 6 minutes. Add the fresh curry leaves followed by the coconut milk and slide in the fish pieces.

Gently simmer till the fish is done (7 to 10 minutes).

Note: You can prepare the sauce ahead of time (prior to adding the curry leaves, coconut milk, and fish) and keep it refrigerated for several days.

Serve with white rice.

Alternative: This sauce is also delicious with prawns.

Green Shrimp

Rajeshwari Pandharipande

Serves 4

For the spice mix

1 green jalapeño pepper
2 tablespoons dry, un-
    sweetened coconut
    flakes

1 tablespoon lemon
    juice
1 teaspoon cumin seed
2 large sprigs cilantro

Grind the ingredients listed above to make a paste.

For the curry

1 pound shrimp
1 teaspoon oil
1 bay leaf
½ onion, finely chopped

½ small tomato,
    chopped
Spice paste as above
½ teaspoon garam
    masala (optional)

Peel and devein the shrimp. Set aside.

Heat the oil on medium. Add the bay leaf and stir for a few seconds. Add the chopped onion and fry till dark brown.

Add the tomato and the spice paste and stir for 5 to 7 minutes on low heat, until the mixture thickens to make a sauce. Add the shrimp and sauté for 5 minutes.

Cover and cook for 10 minutes on low heat.

Add garam masala (if using) and warm for 2 minutes.

Parsi Shrimp Curry

Soli Mistry

Editor's note: The Parsis are a Zoroastrian community from ancient Persia who originally migrated to Gujarat in western India in the 10th century CE and are particularly associated with Bombay (now Mumbai). They have their own specialized food traditions.

Serves 4

25 large shrimp
1 onion finely chopped
6 dried red chillies
1 teaspoon coriander seeds
1 tablespoon coconut flakes
2 tablespoons vegetable oil or ghee (clarified butter)

½ teaspoon turmeric
1½ cups water
½ teaspoon salt
2 teaspoons lemon juice
1 cup canned coconut milk (or "lite" coconut milk if you prefer)

Peel, clean, and devein the shrimp. Set aside. Grind half the chopped onion, red chillies, coriander seeds, and coconut flakes to make a masala paste.

In a pan, heat the oil or ghee and fry the remaining onions until lightly golden. Remove the onions and set aside. In the same oil, fry the masala paste and turmeric, adding a little water if necessary.

Add the fried onions and shrimp to the masala paste and mix together. Add 1½ cups water and the salt, and cook until on low until the shrimp is almost ready. (Be careful not to overcook.) Add the lemon juice and coconut milk to the mixture and continue cooking on low until the shrimp is done.

Serve with white rice, papadums (see glossary), and kachubar (see *Salads.*)

Baked Masala Fish

Aparna Rahman

Serves 4–6

3 tablespoons oil
1 onion, chopped
1 teaspoon garlic, finely chopped
1 teaspoon fresh ginger, finely chopped
¼ teaspoon ground cumin
½ teaspoon ground coriander
½ teaspoon red chilli powder
¼ teaspoon turmeric
½ teaspoon salt or to taste
1 12-ounce can of chopped tomatoes
⅔ cup of barbecue sauce
2 pounds tilapia fillets

Preheat oven to 350 degrees F.

In a frying pan, heat the oil on medium. Brown the onions and add the ginger and garlic. Fry on medium until light brown. Add the cumin, coriander, red chilli powder, turmeric, and salt and stir.

Add the canned tomatoes and cook on medium till the tomatoes become a sauce. Mix in the barbecue sauce.

Arrange the fish in a baking dish in a single layer. Pour the mixture over the fish and bake uncovered for 30 minutes.

Serve with rice or bread.

Whole Baked Fish

Nancy Zutshi

Serves 4–6

4 whole trout or white fish
½ cup olive or grape seed oil
2 teaspoons garam masala
½–¾ teaspoon red chilli pepper
¾ teaspoon turmeric
3 teaspoons paprika
Salt to taste

4 large banana peppers, cut into thick slices
2 large potatoes, peeled and cut crosswise into 1½ inch thick slices
1 medium lemon
1 large red onion chopped fine and refrigerated in cold water

Preheat oven to 350 degrees F.

Wash and clean the fish, removing the heads. Pat dry with paper towels and set aside. Brush a shallow baking pan with a thin layer of oil.

In a large bowl, mix the oil and powdered spices (garam masala, red chilli powder, turmeric, and paprika), salt, and oil to make a paste. Coat each piece of fish inside and out with the reserved spice paste. Arrange fish widthwise in the pan, about 3 inches apart. Save about 2 tablespoons of spice paste. Layer the banana peppers and potatoes between the fish.

Add about 2 tablespoons of olive oil and fresh lemon juice to the remaining paste and drizzle it over all the contents in the pan.

Bake the fish uncovered on the middle rack for approximately an hour. Before serving, sprinkle with chopped onion. This dish can be enjoyed with white rice or naan (see *Breads*).

Bombay INDIAN GRILL

302 S. First St. • 217-398-8400
401 E. Green St. • Campustown
217-344-3380

SP27107

Kukreti Real Estate Services

For All of Your Real Estate Needs

MUKESH KUKRETI
REALTOR®

217-898-5100 **Mobile**
217-355-1400 **Residence**
217-351-7222 **Fax**
mukesh.kukreti@gmail.com
www.**cbHonig-Bell**.com

FOR YOUR RESIDENTIAL OR COMMERCIAL
PURCHASE / SALE / MANAGEMENT / NEW CONSTRUCTION / RENTAL NEEDS
SPECIALIZING IN R.E.I.T. (REAL ESTATE INVESTMENT TRUSTS) TAX BENEFITS
OFFERING 8–15% RETURN ON YOUR INVESTMENTS – GUARANTEED BY COLLATERAL
PRE-FORECLOSURES • FORECLOSURES • DISTRESSED SALES • BANK OWNED PROPERTIES

We Never Stop Moving...
COLDWELL BANKER
HONIG-BELL

ℭℜ

Poultry

In India, poultry recipes would not traditionally include turkey as does this collection, simply because turkey is not native to India. But other poultry—duck and goose—are available; and partridge, quail, and pheasant used to be popular with families that had a hunting tradition. However, for non-vegetarians, chicken has traditionally been considered the most special. Although more affordable today, chicken has not lost its status as a special-occasion food. In North India, it is often associated with Moghul (Mughlai) cooking—the food of kings. Until the 1980s, chicken was not available in neat packages, frozen or refrigerated. Chickens (or fowl) were bred in yards or other outdoor facilities. Thus, they were more muscular and less fatty, and definitely more flavorful. Cooking chicken took much longer when I was growing up than it does today, when the chicken goes from cage to table within a few weeks. As in all Indian meat cooking, the fat is trimmed off the bird wherever possible, and the skin always removed.

Chicken Curry (1)

Braj Kachru

Contributor's note: The ground spices and salt are approximate amounts; adjust according to your taste. Cooking time: About 30–35 minutes.

Serves 6–8

1 packet chicken legs
(6–8 pieces)
1 packet chicken thighs
(6–8 pieces)
4 tablespoons canola or
olive oil
4 or 5 bay leaves
6 cloves
6 green cardamom pods
1 black cardamom,*
broken so seeds are
visible (optional)
2 pieces cinnamon, each
1 inch long
2 medium onions,
chopped fine

½ teaspoon turmeric
½ teaspoon red cayenne
pepper
1½ teaspoons ground
cumin
1½ teaspoons ground
coriander
½ teaspoon ginger pow-
der
1½ teaspoons salt or to
taste
2 large tomatoes,
chopped fine
Garnish: A few sprigs of
fresh cilantro (option-
al)

* **See glossary**

Wash and skin the chicken pieces. Set aside.

In a large nonstick pan, heat the oil on medium heat; add the bay leaves, cloves, cardamom(s) and cinnamon, and fry for a few seconds.

Add the chopped onions and fry till golden brown. Add the turmeric, pepper, cumin, coriander, and ginger and fry for a couple of minutes.

Add the chicken pieces and salt. Stir and mix well. Cover and cook for a couple of minutes. Stir. Repeat the cover-and-cook-and-stir process for ten minutes.

Add the tomatoes slowly, a few spoonfuls at a time, to make a gravy. It will take about 10 to 12 minutes to add all of the tomatoes.

Cover and let simmer for 10 to 15 minutes or so on lower heat. Stir a few times to make sure the chicken does not stick to the bottom and burn. Turn off the heat when chicken is fully cooked.

Garnish with chopped fresh cilantro before serving.

Serve with rice or naan (See *Breads*).

Chicken Curry (2)

Krishna Bhowmik

Serves 4–6

2 pounds chicken (legs, thighs, and breasts)
6 tablespoons canola oil
3 large onions, finely chopped
7 cloves garlic, finely chopped
¼ cup fresh ginger, finely chopped
1 tablespoon ground coriander
1½ teaspoons ground cumin
1 teaspoon ground cardamom seeds
1 teaspoon turmeric
1½ teaspoons garam masala
2 teaspoons red chilli powder
5 tomatoes, diced, or one 8-ounce can of tomato sauce
2–3 cinnamon sticks
5 whole cloves
3 bay leaves
3 cups water
Salt to taste
Garnish: Chopped fresh cilantro

Skin, wash and dry the chicken. Cut the breasts into 3-inch pieces.

In a heavy pan, heat 3 tablespoons of oil over medium heat. Add the chopped onion, and fry until onions are light brown. Add the garlic, ginger, and the ground spices (coriander, cumin, cardamom, turmeric, garam masala, and red chilli powder) and cook for about 2 minutes.

Add tomatoes and cook until the curry sauce is thick and the oil separates from the mixture. Set aside.

In another heavy pan, heat 3 tablespoons of canola oil over medium heat. Add the chicken, cinnamon sticks, whole cloves, and bay leaves. Stir for about 4 to 5 minutes and reduce the heat to low until the chicken is browned. Add the curry sauce, along with 3 cups of water and salt.

Cover and cook on low heat for about 15 minutes until the temperature within the thickest part of the chicken is 160 degrees F. on a meat thermometer, and the meat is tender.

Garnish with fresh chopped cilantro and serve with rice or Indian bread.

Chicken Curry with Coconut

Ania Loomba

Serves 4

For the dry masala

1 teaspoon cumin seeds

1 teaspoon black pep-
percorns

2 tablespoons coriander
seeds

1-inch stick cinnamon

6 cloves

3–4 green cardamom
pods

½ teaspoon fennel seeds

1 tablespoon poppy
seeds (optional)

Combine the spices and roast till they are aromatic. Grind and bottle when cool.

For the chicken curry

2 pounds chicken (legs,
thighs, and breasts)

3 tablespoons of canola
oil

1 medium red onion,
chopped

1 teaspoon fresh ginger,
chopped

1 teaspoon garlic,
chopped

A few fresh curry leaves,
if available

1 tablespoon tomato
paste

½ teaspoon turmeric

½ teaspoon red chilli
flakes

Salt to taste

2–3 tablespoons dry ma-
sala mix (as above)

1 cup yogurt, beaten
smooth

2 tablespoons dried co-
conut powder or 1 cup
coconut milk

Fresh cilantro if curry
leaves are not avail-
able

Wash and skin the chicken. Cut the breasts into 3-inch pieces.

In a large pot, heat the oil on medium heat and add the chopped onion. Fry until brown. Add the ginger and garlic, and sauté lightly for about 3 to 4 minutes. If using fresh curry leaves, add them now and fry.

Add the tomato paste; add the chicken pieces and fry for about 5 to 10 minutes till all sides are coated. Add turmeric and red chilli, salt, and the roasted masala mix. Fry 5 to 10 minutes. Then add the yogurt and dried coconut powder (or the coconut milk).

If you did not use curry leaves, add fresh cilantro at the end and mix well.

Braised Chicken in Rich Sauce
(Chicken Korma)

Padma Reddy

Contributor's note: Born to a vegetarian family and being a vegetarian until I was in my mid-twenties, I had to learn and experiment with preparing meat and poultry dishes on my own when I chose to become a non-vegetarian. I cannot tell you the origin of this recipe since it has evolved in my kitchen, becoming a concoction of various things I like from both North and South India. However, it's very popular with all my Western and Eastern friends, and I do get special requests to make it.

Serves 4–6

1 whole chicken, or 2½ pounds, parts of your choice
(bone or boneless depending on preference)

For the marinade
3 tablespoons yogurt
1½ teaspoons salt
¼ teaspoon turmeric

———————

For the coconut paste
2 teaspoons poppy seeds
⅓ cup dry grated unsweetened coconut
6 whole cashews
2 tablespoons blanched, slivered almonds
3–4 tablespoons water

———————

For the korma
4 tablespoons oil
½ teaspoon mustard seeds
½ piece cinnamon stick
3 whole green cardamom pods
3–4 cloves
1 bay leaf
2 medium onions
2 green chillies, chopped
1½ inch piece fresh ginger (or 2 teaspoons ginger paste)
5 cloves garlic (or 2 teaspoons garlic paste)
3–4 sprigs fresh cilantro

¼ teaspoon turmeric
Red chilli powder to
  taste
1 teaspoon salt
½–¾ cup water
1 teaspoon garam
  masala

1 teaspoon ground cori-
  ander
2 teaspoons lemon or
  lime juice
Garnish: Almond slivers,
  dry-roasted or fried in
  1 teaspoon butter (op-
  tional) & cilantro

Pre-cooking

Marinating: Remove the skin and cut the chicken into 1-inch pieces. Wash and drain. Mix the chicken, yogurt, salt, and turmeric in a bowl and let the chicken marinate for an hour or more.

Making the coconut paste: Grind the poppy seeds to a fine powder. Add the coconut, cashews, and almonds to the poppy-seed powder and grind further to a fine paste, adding water at the very end.

Chopping and grinding: Chop the onions. If using whole fresh ginger and garlic, peel and chop; then grind to a paste. Chop the green chillies and cilantro. Set aside.

Cooking

Heat the oil in a large saucepan on medium heat. When hot, add the mustard seeds, cinnamon sticks, cardamom pods, cloves, and bay leaf.

When the mustard seeds start popping, add the diced onions and chopped green chillies. Sauté the onions until translucent or slightly golden brown. Add the ginger-garlic paste and most of the chopped cilantro (save some for the garnish). After frying for a minute, add the turmeric, red chilli powder, and salt, and stir.

Add the marinated chicken and stir well. Cover and cook on medium-low to medium heat, stirring occasionally. Cook until the chicken turns white.

Add the coconut paste and ½ to ¾ cup water to the chicken and let it simmer on medium-low for 4 to 5 minutes until the sauce thickens and the oil rises to the top.

Add the garam masala and ground coriander. Let the mixture cook for another 2 minutes; then turn off the heat. Add 2 teaspoons of lemon or lime juice and stir.

If you wish, garnish with remaining cilantro and roasted almond slivers before serving.

This dish is best with warm rotis (chapatis, parathas, or puris) or rice.

Chicken Tikka Masala
(Spicy Broiled Chicken Kababs)

Manisha Bhagwat

Editor's note: Some dishes are so well known by their Indian names that it is almost sacrilege to substitute a translation. This is one of those dishes. Widely popular, chicken tikka masala has even infiltrated pub fare in Britain and is served as a sandwich with baguette.

Serves 6–8

2 pounds chicken tenderloins or skinless, boneless breasts of chicken cut into bite-size pieces
¾ cup white vinegar
2 teaspoons salt

For the marinade

2 teaspoons red chilli powder

2 teaspoons ground fresh garlic

2 teaspoons ground fresh ginger

2 teaspoons dry fenugreek leaves (kasoori methi)*

2 teaspoons fresh chopped mint or 1 teaspoon dried mint

½ teaspoon ground cumin

1 teaspoon ground coriander

¼ teaspoon ground black pepper

¼ teaspoon ground cinnamon

⅛ teaspoon ground clove

⅛ teaspoon green cardamom seeds, ground

¼ teaspoon dry mustard

½ teaspoon cumin seeds

1 tablespoon oil

¼ cup yogurt

See glossary. Available at Indian and international food and grocery stores.

Mix the chicken pieces with the vinegar and salt and let stand for 30 minutes.

To marinate

Combine all the ingredients in a blender or food processor and grind as smoothly as possible.

Drain the chicken well and give it a quick cold-water rinse. Dab with paper towels to remove excess water.

Mix chicken pieces well with the marinade, cover, and refrigerate for at least 2 hours. Marinating the chicken for a day or overnight will further enhance the flavor.

To cook

Set the broiler on high.

Thread the pieces onto skewers and broil for 12 to 15 minutes until the chicken is done. Turn the chicken a couple of times.

Arrange on a serving platter and garnish with chopped fresh cilantro, lemon wedges, and red onion rings.

Alternative method: Preheat oven to 425 degrees F. Place the chicken pieces on a wire rack over a roasting pan and cook for 20 to 30 minutes until completely done.

Serve with cumin rice (p. 194) or pullao and cucumber raita (p. 244).

Hint: This chicken can also be served as an appetizer.

Chilli Chicken

Gullapudi Raman Kumari

Editor's note: Most of the oil in this dish is drained after the first step.

Serves 4–6

1 whole chicken
3 teaspoons soy sauce
8 green chillies, 4 mashed and, for later, 4 sliced in rounds
4 teaspoons ginger and garlic paste*
5 teaspoons vinegar
½ teaspoon turmeric
3 tablespoons cornstarch or arrowroot powder
1 tablespoon all-purpose flour
1 teaspoon garam masala
Salt to taste

2 big onions
1 cup oil for shallow frying
3–4 large cloves garlic, minced
1-inch piece of fresh ginger, minced
6–8 fresh curry leaves (optional)
1 teaspoon ground cumin
1 teaspoon ground coriander
1 teaspoon red chilli powder
Garnish: Chopped fresh cilantro (optional)

*Bottled ginger and garlic pastes are available either individually or in combination in Indian and international food and grocery stores.

Wash and skin the chicken. Cut into 1-inch pieces, leaving the bone in.

In a large bowl, mix the chicken cubes with soy sauce, the 4 mashed chillies, ginger and garlic paste, vinegar, turmeric, cornstarch, flour, garam masala and salt. Marinate for at least half an hour.

Slice the onions into thin rings. Set aside.

Heat the oil on medium-high in a large frying pan or wok. Shallow-fry the marinated chicken batch by batch.

Remove the pan from the heat and pour off the oil. Put the minced garlic and ginger and curry leaves (if using) in the pan and return the pan to the heat. Sauté a little to coat with oil.

Add the sliced green chilli and onion rings and the chicken. Add the ground cumin, coriander, and red chilli and stir.

Sauté till the onions become translucent. Remove from the heat. The chicken should not have any liquid but should be juicy. Serve promptly.

Garnish with cilantro.

Chicken Stir-Fry with Vegetables

Nandini Pai

Serves 6–8

For the marinade

½ teaspoon red chilli powder

1 teaspoon ground coriander

1 teaspoon ground cumin

1 tablespoon ginger paste*

1 tablespoon garlic paste*

2 teaspoons vinegar

Salt to taste

1 tablespoon lemon juice

¾ cup yogurt

*Bottled ginger and garlic pastes are available either individually or in combination at Indian and international food and grocery stores.

———

2 pounds chicken tenderloins

1 large onion

2 bell peppers

2 carrots

½ cup sliced mushrooms

1–2 tablespoons oil

Cut the chicken into 1½ inch pieces and set aside.

Make a paste of the marinade ingredients and mix with yogurt. Coat the chicken pieces and marinate overnight or for at least 3 to 4 hours.

Cut the onions, peppers and carrots into 1-inch pieces and set aside with the sliced mushrooms.

In a stir-fry pan, heat the oil on very high and fry the chicken pieces for 5 to 6 minutes until cooked through. Remove the pieces and set aside.

Fry the vegetables in the same frying pan for 2 to 3 minutes until crisp. Combine the vegetables with the chicken before serving.

Hint: You can grill the chicken and avoid using the oil.

Serve with Indian bread.

Broiled Chicken Breasts with Tandoori Masala

Zarina Hock

Contributor's note: This is a quick and easy recipe despite the long list of ingredients! See note below.

Serves 4–6

4 skinless chicken breasts

For the marinade

¾ cup yogurt, low-fat or fat-free if you prefer
1 small onion
4 large cloves garlic
1-inch piece of fresh ginger
1 teaspoon ground cumin‡
2 teaspoons ground coriander‡
¼ teaspoon ground cloves‡
¼ teaspoon ground cinnamon‡
½ teaspoon (or to taste) black pepper‡
½ teaspoon green cardamom seeds, crushed‡
½ teaspoon red chilli powder
¼ teaspoon turmeric (for color)
1–2 teaspoons tandoori masala (spice mix)*
1 teaspoon sweet paprika (for color)
Salt to taste
1–2 tablespoons lemon juice
1 tablespoon olive oil
Cooking spray

Garnish:

Red onion, sliced in thin rings
Lemon wedges
Tomatoes
A few sprigs fresh cilantro

*Available at Indian and international food and grocery stores. (Do not overuse since you are adding your own spices anyway.)

‡ You can, if you wish, use 2 teaspoons garam masala instead of these individual spices though the flavor may differ somewhat.

Wash the chicken breasts, remove all fat, and make several ½-inch gashes in the flesh. Set aside.

Whisk the yogurt with a fork and make smooth (not frothy). Pour into a large bowl that has a tight lid. Grind the onions, garlic, and ginger to a smooth paste and add to the yogurt. Mix in all the other spices. Add the salt, lemon juice, and olive oil.

Add the chicken breasts and gently rub in the marinade, making sure the mixture is rubbed into the gashes. (I use disposable vinyl gloves when applying the marinade.) Marinate at least 4 to 6 hours but preferably overnight.

To cook, set the broiler on high. Spray a cookie sheet with olive oil. Take the chicken breasts out of the bowl and gently shake off as much of the excess marinade as possible. Place the breasts on the sheet so they are not touching. Spray the top with olive oil. Set the sheet on the middle rack in the oven. Broil for 10 minutes on each side. The meat should char a little on the edges and should be cooked through.

When the chicken is done, let it cool slightly. Cut lengthwise in slices about 1½ inches wide. Place on a platter.

Garnish with wedges of lemon, tomato, onion slices, and sprigs of cilantro.

Serve with naan (see *Breads*) or tandoori roti (available at Indian and international food and grocery stores).

Hint: For additional "kick," sprinkle with a pinch of ground cumin, pepper, and red chilli powder before serving.

Karachi Ginger Chicken

Zohreh Sullivan

Editor's note: India and Pakistan are both part of the Indian Subcontinent, and the cuisines of North India and Pakistan have much in common.

Serves 4–6

2 pounds chicken (or whole chicken, if small)
½ cup oil
3 inches fresh ginger, chopped fine
4–5 cloves garlic
½ teaspoon red chilli powder

2 tomatoes, chopped
½ cup yogurt
½ cup milk (or, if you prefer, cream)
Salt to taste
⅓ cup ground almonds
Garnish: Chopped fresh cilantro and/or a few curry leaves

Wash, skin, and cut the chicken into serving pieces.

Heat the oil on medium and add the ginger and garlic. Sauté for 3 minutes.

Add the chicken and fry briefly. Add the red chilli powder and then the tomatoes. Cook for 3 minutes. Add the yogurt and milk (or cream) and the salt. Cook for 4 or 5 minutes. Stir in the ground almonds and more milk as desired.

Cover and simmer till the chicken is tender.

Garnish with cilantro and or curry leaves before serving.

Serve with rice or South Asian bread.

Masala Turkey Breast

Hans Henrich Hock

Editor's note: As part of our family's Thanksgiving meal, this dish is served along with the traditional Thanksgiving turkey.

Serves 6–8

5-pound boneless turkey breast skinned*
1 tablespoon black peppercorns
6 or 7 dried red chillies
2 tablespoons green cardamom pods
3 or 4 sticks cinnamon
1 teaspoon cloves
1 6-ounce packet slivered almonds
1 head (whole bulb) garlic, peeled and crushed

1 piece fresh ginger, peeled and crushed (roughly same amount as garlic)
Juice of 1 lemon
1 tablespoon salt (or to taste)
½ cup olive oil (plus about ¼ cup for basting)

*With doneness indicator or meat thermometer

Preheat oven to 300 degrees F.

Rinse the turkey breast in cold water and dry thoroughly.

Finely grind the black peppercorns, red chillies, cardamom pods, cinnamon, and cloves with the almonds. Add the crushed garlic and ginger, lemon juice, salt, and oil. This should make a thick masala paste.

Make slits in the turkey breast with a knife to permit the paste flavors to penetrate. Coat the turkey breast with the masala, making sure to rub the paste into the slits.

Bake turkey on a rack set on a roasting pan, basting occasionally with ¼ cup of olive oil to prevent the turkey and masala from drying out too much. Bake till the thermometer indicates that the turkey is done. Serve sliced with the crusty masala crumbles sprinkled over the slices.

Turkey Meatball Curry
(Kashmiri Style Kofta Curry)

Braj Kachru

Serves 4

1½ teaspoons red cayenne pepper (more if you like it hot)

¾ teaspoon ginger powder

2 teaspoons ground fennel

1 teaspoon ground cumin

2 pinches hing (asafoetida)

3 tablespoons yogurt

3 pods black cardamom* seeds, crushed (save the skins)

1 tablespoon vegetable oil for mixing + 2 tablespoons for frying

1 teaspoon salt or to taste

1½ pounds ground, lean turkey

1 cup water

½ teaspoon garam masala

4 cloves

3 bay leaves

*****See glossary**

In a medium-size bowl, mix together 1 teaspoon cayenne pepper, ½ teaspoon ginger, 1 teaspoon fennel, ½ teaspoon cumin, a pinch of hing, 1 tablespoon yogurt, the crushed black cardamom seeds, 1 tablespoon oil, and half the salt. Knead this mixture with the ground turkey so that all the ingredients are mixed well.

Make 18 equal portions of the turkey mix. On a flat, greased surface, roll each portion gently by hand to make 3-inch long sausage-shaped rolls (koftas). Set aside.

Heat 2 tablespoons of oil in a deep pan. Mix the remaining yogurt and cayenne pepper and add to the oil, stirring briskly. When the oil separates, add the water and stir again.

Add to the pan the remaining ginger, fennel, cumin, and hing, plus the garam masala, cloves, bay leaves, black cardamom skins, and salt. Cook till the gravy comes to a boil.

Carefully slide in the koftas, one at a time, and cook on medium-high heat till the gravy starts to thicken. Lower the heat and cook, stirring gently, till the oil separates.

Serve with rice or naan (see *Breads*).

For additional gravy to go with your rice or naan:
If you like more gravy for your rice or naan, add one finely chopped, medium tomato, 1 teaspoon at a time to the gravy, before sliding in the koftas. Cook for ten minutes after lowering the heat; the koftas will be done though you may not see the oil separate.

Lamb

Although various red meats are eaten in India (depending on the particular religion, social class, or region), the recipes in this collection focus on lamb, which is, interestingly enough, not the preferred red meat in India. What is called *mutton* is the meat most widely used, and this is *not*—as often mistakenly assumed—a cut of leathery and musty old sheep. It is, in fact, goat, and it is lean though not as tender as the meats we find here. It does, however, lend itself well to Indian cuisine because it requires somewhat longer cooking time and has plenty of opportunity to absorb the many aromatic spices used. In the United States, where goat's meat has only recently become available, lamb is substituted for goat. When using lamb, be sure to buy the leanest cut you can find. Indian meat cooking requires trimming the fat off the meat.

Braised Lamb Shanks over Pear & Beet Salad

Indranil Dutta

Contributor's note: Preparation time 10 minutes. Cooking time: 15 minutes for preparing the braising liquid; 2 hours for braising in the oven. Total time: 2 hours, 25 minutes.

Serves 2

2 lamb shanks

For the dry rub

2 tablespoons ground cumin

2 tablespoons Kashmiri mirch* or any red chilli powder

2 tablespoons ground coriander

Salt to taste

2 tablespoons olive oil (extra-virgin)

*See glossary

For the braising liquid

3 tablespoons olive oil (extra-virgin)

2–3 shallots, julienned

2 bay leaves

Salt to taste

5 cloves garlic, roughly chopped

2 tablespoons coriander seeds, coarsely crushed

1 cup red wine (any red wine will do)

2 tomatoes, sliced

1 cup water

5–6 green olives

For searing the meat

2 tablespoons of olive oil

For the salad

1 pear and 1 beetroot cut into ⅛ inch thick triangles.

Preheat oven to 350 degrees F.

"French trim" the lamb shanks. (You can ask the butcher to trim the meat and to make the necessary gashes in the shanks but not detach the meat from the bone.)

Combine the cumin, chilli powder, coriander, salt and oil and coat the lamb shanks so that the rub covers the meat completely. Set aside.

In a heavy-bottomed pan over medium heat, add 2 table-spoons of olive oil and sear the lamb shanks on each side for about 5 minutes. Make sure the color is a bright red. Do not char but make sure the skin and fat are nicely seared. Set aside.

For the braising liquid, in another heavy-bottomed pan heat 3 tablespoons of olive oil on low. Add the shallots and bay leaves. Add the salt and cook uncovered. It is important to "sweat" the shallots so that they remain pink. Adding salt will keep the shallots from caramelizing. The process takes about 5 minutes.

Add the chopped garlic when the shallots start sweating. Add the coarsely ground coriander seeds (this helps release the flavors better than the ground coriander). When the shallots and garlic are soft, deglaze the pan with red wine. Add the 2 sliced tomatoes and a cup of water.

When the tomatoes are semi-cooked, place the seared shanks in an oven-safe braising pan. Pour the braising liquid into the pan, making sure that the liquid covers the shanks. Use additional warm water if required. Add the olives.

Cook in the oven for about 2 hours or till the meat is fork tender.

Before serving, take about 1 cup of the strained braising liquid and in a small saucepan boil it till it is reduced to about 3 to 4 tablespoons.

Serving suggestion: This dish is best enjoyed with plain rice. Serve the rice on a platter. Top with the pear and beetroot wedges placed alternately to form a circle over the rice. Place the lamb shanks alongside and drizzle about 2 tablespoons of the reduced braising liquid over the plate. If insufficient, spoon a little more of the braising liquid over the shanks as necessary.

Lamb Kababs

Soli Mistry

Contributor's note: In the Parsi community, this dish is *always* served with *dhansak* (p. 88) and caramelized rice (see p. 193).

Serves 4

1 pound minced lamb
2 medium onions, chopped fine
6 cloves garlic, chopped fine
¾-inch fresh ginger root, chopped fine

⅔ teaspoon turmeric
3 tablespoons cilantro, chopped fine
2–4 green chillies, chopped fine
1 egg
1¼ teaspoons salt

Preheat oven to 350 degrees F.

Mix all the ingredients with the lamb, forming small kababs (meatballs the size of ping-pong balls), and place in a baking dish lined with foil. Bake for approximately ½ an hour.

Insert a toothpick in the kababs to test for doneness. If the pick comes out clear, the meat is done. Let the kababs brown a little on the outside before removing from oven.

Skewered Lamb Kababs
(Boti Kabab)

Munni Rodrigues

Serves 4–6

3 teaspoon cumin seeds
2 teaspoons black cumin seeds (shah zeera)*
3 green cardamoms (seeds only)
5 teaspoons coriander seeds
1 stick of cinnamon, about 2 inches long
6 cloves
2 "petals" star anise*
1 teaspoon mustard seeds
3 teaspoons white poppy seeds (this serves as a thickener)
½ cup olive oil

*See glossary

1 head of garlic (a whole bulb), peeled and crushed
3 tablespoons fresh-crushed fresh ginger
1 teaspoon black pepper
1 teaspoon cayenne pepper (or to taste)
1–2 teaspoons salt
2 tablespoons lemon juice
½ cup unflavored yogurt
2 pounds lean lamb, cut into 1-inch cubes
Garnish: 1 medium red onion, sliced into paper-thin rings

In a spice grinder, grind to a powder all the whole spices (regular cumin, black cumin, cardamom seeds, coriander seeds, cinnamon stick, cloves, star anise, mustard seeds, and poppy seeds).

In a blender or food processor, combine the oil, garlic, and ginger and blend smooth. Add the fresh ground spices as well as the black and cayenne pepper, salt, and lemon juice. Blend to make a thick paste.

In a large bowl, stir the yogurt till it is smooth (do not whip). Mix the spice paste with the yogurt, and add the meat cubes, coating them completely.

Cover and marinate the meat in the refrigerator for 6 to 8 hours.

Prepare the grill or set the oven on broil.

Thread the meat on skewers. Position the meat 4 to 5 inches from the heat. Grill (or broil) for 7 to 10 minutes on each side, till the meat is browned and cooked through.

Garnish with onion rings and serve with Indian bread.

Parsi Style Lamb & Lentil Curry
(Dhansak)

Soli Mistry

Contributor's note: Dhansak, or Meat and Lentil Curry, is the signature dish of the Parsis, a Zoroastrian community from Persia who migrated to India in the 10th century CE. Each Parsi family has its own recipe for *dhansak,* which is traditionally enjoyed for Sunday lunch. The dish consists of dal cooked with pieces of lamb. It is always served with caramelized rice (p. 193), kababs (p. 85), and a salad-style dish called *kachubar* (p. 236).

Serves 4–6

2 cups red lentils
8 cups water
1 teaspoon salt
1 large onion, chopped
2 large cloves garlic, chopped
1 tablespoon fresh ginger, chopped
4 tablespoons butter
1 heaping tablespoon dhansak masala (a powdered spice blend available at Indian groceries)
1 tablespoon apple vinegar
1 pound lamb cubed for stew
Garnish: Chopped fresh cilantro

Wash the lentils and drain. Put the water with the lentils in a saucepan with, salt, onion, garlic, ginger, and butter. Boil on medium heat, stirring from time to time, until the lentils are completely cooked and smooth.

Add the dhansak masala a little at a time, stirring continuously (to avoid clumping), along with the vinegar. Once the dal is cooked and has a smooth texture, add the lamb pieces and cook until the meat is tender.

Garnish with fresh coriander.

Braised Lamb in Rich Sauce
(Lamb Korma)

Indranil Dutta

Adapted and reprinted with permission from Tulsi Dharma-rajan's blog, http://tulsid.wordpress.com/category/food/.

Serves 4–6

In a food grinder or blender, separately combine the ingredients for each of the pastes and blend each till smooth.

Paste #1
3 tablespoons garlic paste
3 tablespoons ginger paste
3 green chillies

Paste #2
1 cup yogurt
½ teaspoon turmeric
1 teaspoon red chilli powder
3 tomatoes chopped
Salt to taste

Paste #3
1 cup grated coconut
4 teaspoons fennel seeds
2 teaspoons poppy seeds

———

For the korma
2 pounds lamb
3 tablespoons oil
3 cinnamon sticks
6 green cardamom pods
2 star anise
A few whole black peppercorns
6 cloves
1½ large red onions, sliced

Trim the fat off the lamb and cut into cubes. Set aside.

In a medium pot, heat the oil on medium-high. Put in the cinnamon sticks, cardamom pods, star anise, peppercorns, and cloves. When these begin to puff up and smell fragrant, add the sliced onions. When the onions turn slightly golden, add paste #1. Keep stirring.

When the onions turn soft, add the meat and cook over medium heat till the juices are released from the meat. Then add paste #2 and cook about 30 minutes.

Finally, add paste #3 and cook until the meat is fully cooked.

Note: You may need to add some water between the steps if the mixture starts sticking to the bottom.

Serve with rice or Indian bread.

Lamb Korma in Cashew Masala

Manisha Bhagwat

Serves 4–6

For the cashew masala

1 ounce raw unsalted cashew nuts

3–6 dry red chillies (remove the seeds if you prefer; I use them whole)

2–2¼ inch piece of fresh ginger

1 cup water

2-inch stick of cinnamon

¼ teaspoon green cardamom seeds

3–5 cloves

1½ tablespoons garlic paste

2 tablespoons white poppy seeds*

1 tablespoon coriander seeds

1 teaspoon cumin seeds

*Available at Indian and international food and grocery stores. **See glossary.**

For the korma

1½ pounds skinless, boneless leg of lamb

6 tablespoons ghee (clarified butter) or olive oil

½ pound very finely cut onions

2 teaspoons salt

½ cup yogurt

¼ teaspoon saffron powder

½ cup water

2 tablespoons fresh green cilantro, chopped

1 tablespoon lemon juice

First prepare the cashew masala. In a blender or food processor, grind the cashew nuts, chillies, and ginger with 1 cup of water. Add the remaining masala ingredients and grind thoroughly to make a smooth paste.

Trim the fat and cut the lamb into 2-inch cubes. Set aside.

Heat the ghee/olive oil over medium heat and sauté the onions till golden brown. Add the salt, cashew masala, and yogurt and fry until the ghee/oil forms a film on the top. Keep stirring often.

Add the meat and saffron to this mixture. Add ½ cup of water. Cover the pot and let the meat simmer on low heat for 20 to 25 minutes.

Add 1 tablespoon cilantro and mix well. Cover the pot and cook for another 10 minutes till the meat is tender.

Pour the lamb korma into a serving bowl, and stir in the lemon juice. Top with the remaining tablespoon of fresh cilantro.

Serve with cumin rice (p. 194) or pullao (see *Rice*), or with traditional bread such as naan, chapati, or tandoori roti (see *Breads*).

Alternative: This dish can also be made with skinless, boneless breast of chicken.

Kashmiri Lamb Curry in Rich Sauce with Mint Chutney

(Kashmiri Rogan Josh)

Nancy Zutshi

Contributor's note: This is my own modification of Kashmiri Rogan Josh, which I have improvised over the years. Serve with mint chutney.

Serves 6–8

3 pounds lean lamb loin chops or 3-inch cubes of leg of lamb, bone intact (leave a bit of the fat intact)
2 tablespoons olive oil
1 tablespoon sugar
½ teaspoon hing (asafoetida)
1–2 cloves garlic, minced fine
2–3 bay leaves
5–7 green cardamom pods
1 cinnamon stick
1 teaspoon cumin seeds
½ teaspoon cayenne pepper
1 tablespoon paprika
1 teaspoon ginger powder
½ teaspoon salt or to taste
1 cup cold water
½ teaspoon ground nutmeg

Wash the meat, drain as much as possible, and pat dry. In a deep pan, heat the oil on moderately high heat. Add the sugar, and as it starts to turn brown, add the hing, garlic, and meat. Close the lid, and after a minute or so carefully remove the lid and stir the meat, coating it on all sides with the browned sugar.

Add the bay leaves, cardamom, cinnamon stick, and whole cumin, and stir for another minute. Turn the heat to medium-low and add all the remaining spices except the nutmeg, along with 1 cup of cold water.

Cover and bring to a boil. Turn the heat to low and simmer for 1 hour, gently stirring occasionally, until a very thick gravy is forms. Skim off the excess oil and add the nutmeg.

For the mint chutney

1 bunch of fresh green
   mint, washed
½ cup walnuts or
   pecans

½ cup yogurt
Dash of red pepper
Salt to taste

Blend all the ingredients and serve as a condiment with the lamb.

.

Lamb Smothered in Onion Gravy
(Do Piaza)

Tasneem F. Husain

Serves 6

2 pounds lamb (hind legs with bone), cubed*

4 tablespoons oil

3 medium onions, chopped

2 teaspoons ginger paste

1 teaspoon garlic paste

1 teaspoon salt or to taste

1 teaspoon red chilli powder or to taste

¼ teaspoon turmeric

1 or 2 chopped green chillies (optional)

¼ cup of water

3 rhubarb stalks, chopped (if not in season, 2 tablespoons lemon juice)

1 teaspoon black pepper

Chopped cilantro for garnish

* You can ask the butcher to cube the lamb.

This recipe uses a pressure cooker, but directions for non-pressure cooking are provided at the end.

In a pressure cooker
Put the lamb, oil, chopped onions, ginger and garlic pastes, salt, red chilli powder, turmeric, chopped green chillies (if using) with the water into a pressure cooker. When the pressure cooker indicates that it has reached its high point (usually with a whistle), reduce the heat to low and cook for ten minutes.

Remove from the heat and wait till it is safe to open the cooker. The meat should be tender and the onions should have disintegrated to make a thick gravy. If using rhubarb, add now and cook gently until it blends in with the gravy. It will soften and combine very quickly. If you are not using rhubarb, add the lemon juice and mix it in. Sprinkle in the black pepper and stir.

In a heavy pot
If not using a pressure cooker, follow the same process using a heavy pot. Bring the meat and spices to a boil using ½ to ¾ cups of water. Lower the heat to medium, and cover and cook for 30 minutes until the meat is tender, the onions have disintegrated, and the gravy is thick. Add the rhubarb and cook till it blends in. (Alternatively, add the lemon juice.) If the gravy is too thick, add a little more water and simmer.

In both methods of cooking, the key to doneness is the gravy—it should be thick and the oil should separate from the solids.

Garnish with chopped cilantro. Serve with rice or roti.

Minced Lamb

(Lamb Keema)

Murtaza Husain

Editor's note: A quick and easy dish to make, this is one of the first foods that non-vegetarian Indian and Pakistani students learn to make when they are desperate for home cooking!

Serves 4–5

3 tablespoons oil
2 medium onions, chopped
1 teaspoon ginger paste
1 teaspoon garlic paste
1 teaspoon cayenne pepper
1 teaspoon salt
Pinch of turmeric
1 pound ground lamb
1 medium tomato, chopped
2 tablespoons chopped cilantro stems
½ cup frozen peas, thawed (optional)
1 small potato, cut into small pieces (optional)
2 tablespoons chopped cilantro leaves
1 tablespoon lemon juice (or to taste)

In a saucepan, heat the oil and sauté the onions till they turn brown. Add the ginger and garlic pastes, cayenne pepper, salt, and turmeric and stir.

Add the ground meat and continue stirring to break up the lumps. When the colors changes, add chopped cilantro stems and chopped tomatoes. Cover and cook for 10 to 15 minutes.

If using a chopped potato, add now and stir. Cook on low till potato is done. Add the peas (if using) and simmer for 5 to 7 minutes. Add lemon juice and cilantro leaves.

Serve with rice or chapati. Pocket breads filled with keema are great for lunches and picnics.

ℜ
Eggs

Eggs are an important source of protein, especially for those vegetarians who eat eggs (there are some vegetarians who do not). Eggs at breakfast are often prepared in ways similar to the West, though Indian-style omelettes have acquired a distinctive character and are a popular breakfast food. They are spicy, of course, and in Indian restaurants will often be served with ketchup on the side. Egg curries are popular in home cooking. And in the region known as Awadh in North India, Nargisi Koftas— eggs individually wrapped in spiced ground meat and cooked in a rich sauce—are part of the elegant cuisine of Awadh's courtiers, who were famed for their food and their *tehzeeb* (culture).

Quick & Tasty Eggs

Gullapudi Raman Kumari

Serves 4

6 eggs
4–5 teaspoons oil
2 large red onions, sliced
  into half-rings
6-8 curry leaves, cut into
  thin pieces
¾-inch piece fresh gin-
  ger, crushed
6 big cloves garlic
  crushed
½ teaspoon turmeric
1 teaspoon red chilli
  powder
Salt to taste

Hard boil the eggs with salt. When they are done and cooled, shell them and slice each in half.

Heat a skillet over medium heat and then add the oil. Add the onions and fry until translucent. Add the curry leaves and crushed ginger and garlic. Fry till the mixture loses its raw smell.

Add the turmeric, red chilli powder, and salt. Stir to combine the ingredients and sauté briefly. Place the egg halves in the mixture, yolk-side facing down. Heat for 1 minute; then remove.

The eggs are good with plain rice and dal or Indian bread. They can also be used as fillers in sandwiches or croissants.

Egg Curry with Coconut

Manisha Bhagwat

Serves 3–4

6 eggs
1–2 teaspoons oil + 1 tablespoon oil
2 medium onions, finely chopped (divided into two batches)
¼ cup dry grated coconut (unsweetened)
1½ teaspoons chopped garlic
1 teaspoon chopped fresh ginger
2–3 whole cloves
4–6 whole black peppercorns
1-inch cinnamon stick
2–3 teaspoons red chilli powder
¼ teaspoon turmeric
1 tablespoon garam masala
½ teaspoon ground fennel
1½ cups water
Salt to taste
Garnish: 1–2 tablespoons finely chopped fresh cilantro

Boil the eggs for 10 minutes. Cool and peel.

In a pan, heat 1 to 2 teaspoons oil. Add 1 chopped onion to the pan and sauté till light brown. Add the dry coconut and fry till light brown. Remove from heat. In a blender or food processor, grind the fried onions and coconut with the garlic and ginger and a small amount of water.

In a 3-quart pan, heat 1 tablespoon oil and add the cloves, black peppercorns, and cinnamon stick. Add the remaining chopped onions and sauté.

Add the coconut-onion paste, followed by the red chilli powder, turmeric, garam masala, and ground fennel. Sauté for 1 minute and then add 1½ cups water and salt to taste. Bring to a boil.

Cut a few small gashes into each of the eggs and gently set them in the gravy. Sprinkle fresh cilantro on top.

Cover and turn the heat off.

Serve with fresh chapatis or plain rice.

Egg Curry with Tomatoes

Manisha Bhagwat

Serves 3–4

6 eggs
2 tablespoons oil
2 medium onions, ground
1 teaspoon garlic paste
1 teaspoon ginger paste
2 medium tomatoes, ground
2½ teaspoons red chilli powder
¼ teaspoon turmeric
1 tablespoon garam masala
2 cups water
Salt to taste
1 tablespoon fresh chopped cilantro
2 teaspoons fresh chopped mint leaves

Boil the eggs for 10 minutes. Cool and peel.

In a 3-quart pan, heat 1 tablespoon oil and fry the ground onions till deep brown. Add the garlic and ginger pastes and fry till the oil separates from the solids.

Add the ground tomatoes, red chilli powder, turmeric, and garam masala. Sauté till almost dry. Add 2 cups of water and salt to taste and bring to a boil.

Cut a few small gashes into each of the eggs and gently set them in this spicy, fragrant gravy.

Sprinkle with chopped cilantro and mint leaves. Cover the pan and turn the heat off.

Variations: You can add boiled and lightly roasted potatoes to the curry and/or cooked green peas.

Serve with fresh chapatis or basmati rice.

Fusion Egg & Vegetable Curry

Margrith Mistry

Serves 4–6

6 eggs
1 tablespoon vegetable or olive oil
1 teaspoon black mustard seeds
1 medium onion, chopped
3 cloves of garlic, crushed or chopped (more if you like)
1 tablespoon commercial curry paste* (or more if you wish)

Seasonal vegetables: 1 green pepper and 1 red pepper, cut into bite-size squares, 2 medium zucchinis, peeled and sliced, and any other vegetable you enjoy
1 cup plain yogurt (more if you increase the vegetables)
Salt to taste

*Available at Indian or international food and grocery stores.

Hard-boil the eggs, shell, and cut into halves.

In a frying pan, heat the oil on medium and fry the mustard seeds until they pop. Add the onions and garlic and sauté briefly. Add the curry paste and the eggs, and cook until the eggs are lightly coated.

In the meantime, cook the vegetables in the microwave (or a stovetop steamer) till tender but not mushy.

Transfer the vegetables to the frying pan and mix lightly with the eggs and curry paste. Add a little water (about 2 tablespoons) and cook gently.

Let cool. Gently stir in the yogurt and warm lightly before serving. (Boiling will curdle the yogurt.)

Masala Omelette

Hans Henrich Hock

Serves 1–2

2 eggs (or 2 egg whites)
Pinch of salt and black pepper
Pinch of red pepper (optional)
1¼ teaspoons olive oil
1 tablespoon finely cut onion

1 teaspoon finely cut green chilli
1 teaspoon chopped cilantro
¼ teaspoon ground cumin (optional)

Beat the eggs together with the salt and the black and red pepper (if using), and set aside.

In a heavy frying pan or an iron griddle, heat 1 teaspoon of oil over medium heat. When the oil is warm, arrange the mix of chopped onion, green chilli, and cilantro in a ridge down the middle of the pan, sprinkling the surface of the mixture with the remaining oil. Pour the beaten eggs over the mixture and sprinkle with the ground cumin (if using). Reduce the heat to low.

When the egg mixture is beginning to set, fold it over from both sides. Flip it over and fry a bit longer, till golden brown.

Serve with chapati or toast.

Scrambled Eggs to Wake You Up
(Egg Bhujiya)

Munni Rodrigues

Serves 2

4 eggs
1 tablespoon milk
¼ teaspoon ground
  cumin (or less)
1 green chilli, sliced
2 teaspoons chopped
  cilantro
¼ teaspoon black

pepper
¼ teaspoon cayenne
  pepper (or to taste)
2 teaspoons oil
1 tablespoon onion,
  chopped finely
¼ cup chopped tomato
Salt to taste

Mix the eggs (or, if you prefer, just the egg whites) with the milk and all the seasonings except the onion, tomato, and oil. Set aside.

In a skillet, heat the oil over medium heat, and fry the onions and tomato 3 to 4 minutes until the onions turn translucent and the tomatoes soften. Do not allow the tomatoes to give off too much liquid.

Reduce the heat and add the egg mixture and gently cook, stirring, until the eggs begin to curdle and set. Do not overcook or the eggs will become rubbery.

Remove from the heat and serve with chapati or toast.

Egg Casserole

Vidya Tripathy

Editor's note: This casserole requires preparation the day before you bake it.

Serves 4–6

12 eggs (8 whole + 4 egg whites 3 cups milk)
1 teaspoon dry mustard powder
1 teaspoon salt
½ teaspoon black pepper
¼ teaspoon ground cumin
Pinch of red chilli powder, or to taste
2 tablespoons chopped scallions
2 tablespoons chopped cilantro
¼ cup bell peppers, chopped (optional)
½ cup chopped mushrooms (optional)
1 small green chilli, chopped (optional)
2 cups cheddar cheese, grated
6 slices of white bread (remove crust)
Cooking oil spray

The day before baking
Spray a 9-inch x 13-inch baking dish with oil.

Beat 8 eggs with yolks and 4 egg whites together with the milk until frothy. Add the mustard powder, salt, black pepper, ground cumin, red chilli powder, chopped scallions, and chopped cilantro. If using, add bell peppers, mushrooms, and green chilli. Add the cheese and mix well.

Layer the bread in the dish and pour the mixture over it. Cover and refrigerate overnight.

The following day
Preheat oven to 350 degrees F.

Bake the casserole uncovered for 50 minutes to 1 hour, till the mixture is set. Serve hot.

෧

Dals, Beans & Other Legumes

Dals are a major source of protein for those who are vegetarian. The term *dal* is used in India to refer broadly to all kinds of lentils, pulses, and other legumes. Essential and basic to Indian diets, dals express the idiom of sustenance in phrases such as *dal-bhaat* (dal and rice) or *dal-roti* (dal and bread)—equivalent in concept to "daily bread" or "bread and butter" in English. Dals can be comfort foods or very elaborate creations. They can be prepared with or without vegetables and in some cases with meat, as in *dhansak* (p. 88). Since some dals are harder to digest than others, they are often cooked with natural digestive aids such as ginger and asafoetida (hing). Typically, dals are cooked in water (like a soup) often with a few spices and then seasoned with oil and more spices. The "zing" to dal comes from this seasoning process, which is known by various names in India, such as *tarka, baghaar, fodni,* or *chhaunk.* The combination of spices in each tarka will vary.

Since the tarka process appears frequently in the dal section, it will not be referenced each time. For more on tarka, see p. 23 and the glossary. The glossary entry on dals provides the names of several popular dals and general information. Individual dals are listed as separate entries. The Internet is a rich resource for more details.

Dals are traditionally served as a main dish with rice or Indian bread and often with wedges of lemon on the side.

Sprouted Moong Beans

Usha Gandhi

Serves 4–6

2 cups of whole green moong* beans
1 tablespoon oil
½–1 teaspoon black mustard seeds
Pinch of hing (asafoetida)
1 teaspoon finely chopped fresh ginger

¼ teaspoon turmeric
Salt to taste
1 chopped green chilli (optional)
½ teaspoon red chilli powder (optional)
Juice of 1 lime or lemon
Garnish: Chopped fresh cilantro

*Same as *mung*

To sprout the moong beans
Wash and soak the moong in plenty of water for 10 to 14 hours until the beans expand and the outer green skins break open. (It helps sometimes to warm the water slightly before adding it to the moong.) Scoop out the beans from the water with your hand and transfer to a sieve or strainer that is lined with a muslin cloth or a paper towel—or, as a Vietnamese lady taught me—into an unglazed mud pot. (If you find any hard moong beans, separate them and soak a little longer. Do not use them "as is"—they will not sprout and could damage your teeth!)

For the next 24 to 48 hours (depending on the weather and the temperature in the room and on how long you would like the sprouts to be) keep the moong moist by sprinkling them with a few drops of water both morning and evening.

To prepare the dish
Heat the oil in a frying pan on medium-high. Add the mustard seeds and stir. When the seeds start to pop, add the hing. Stir and add the ginger and fry for half a minute before adding the sprouted moong and the turmeric. Sprinkle with a little water (a couple of teaspoons), add salt, and cover and cook for 5 minutes at medium heat, stirring once or twice. (If you would like the moong to be soft rather than crunchy, cook a little longer.)

If using the fresh green chilli and the red chilli powder, add them now.

Add the juice of a lime or lemon, and garnish with cilantro before serving.

Stir-Fried Lentil Sprouts with Fenugreek Leaves

Zarina Hock

Contributor's note: This recipe calls for dried fenugreek leaves, a taste worth cultivating. If you find the flavor too strong, you can omit fenugreek from the dish.

Serves 4–6

½ cup lentil sprouts (brown lentils)

¼ cup dried fenugreek leaves (kasoori methi)*

1 tablespoon olive oil

½ teaspoon mustard seeds

1 small yellow onion, chopped (less, if you wish)

1–2 green chillies, sliced (or red pepper flakes to taste)

Pinch of hing (asafoetida)

¼ teaspoon turmeric

1 tablespoon or more of fresh lemon juice

Salt to taste

*See glossary

To sprout the lentils

Wash the lentils and soak them for 8 hours in a bowl of cold water. Then drain the lentils and put them in a moist kitchen towel in a bowl in a warm place. (I store mine under the kitchen sink.) The towel should be moist, *not* sopping wet.

Check the lentils twice a day. Drain them in cool water once a day and return them to the bowl, making sure that the towel is moist. On the second day, the lentils will begin to sprout. Once the sprouts have grown to about ¼ inch and have expanded to twice their volume, rinse and drain them.

To make the stir-fry
Soak the fenugreek leaves in ¼ cup of water. Chop the onion.

In a karhai (or wok), heat the oil over medium heat, and when hot add the mustard seeds. When these sizzle and pop, stir in the chopped onions.

Fry for a few minutes till the onions go limp and turn slightly brown at the edges. Add the green chillies and fry till they turn bright green and start to release their aroma. (If using red pepper flakes, stir-fry briefly.)

Add the hing and stir rapidly for a couple of seconds; add the turmeric and fenugreek with about 1 tablespoon of the water it has been soaking in. Stir till the water is mostly gone, and then gently add the lentils.

Toss and stir-fry for 3 minutes. Add the lemon juice and salt to taste.

Remove from the heat before the lentil sprouts turn limp.

Serving suggestion: Serve warm or at room temperature. The lentils make a fresh and crunchy accompaniment for most meals. Garnish with whole cherry tomatoes and serve as a salad.

Split Moong Dal

Tulsi Dharmarajan

Editor's note: This basic dal recipe can be used for other dals as well. Adapted and reprinted with permission from the contributor's blog, http://tulsid.wordpress.com/category/food/.

Serves 4

1 cup split moong dal
2–3 cups of water
½ teaspoon salt (or to taste)
1 tablespoon oil
1 teaspoon cumin seeds

3 dried red chillies, broken into large pieces
1 onion, julienned
½ teaspoon turmeric
½ teaspoon ground cumin

Wash the dal thoroughly and drain.

In a medium saucepan, bring the moong dal to a boil in 2 to 3 cups of water, depending on how soupy you want your dal to be. Partially cover and let the dal simmer briskly until it is soft. Stir in the salt.

The tarka
Heat the oil in a small pan. When hot, add the cumin seeds and red chilli pieces. When cumin seeds begin to sputter, add the onions. When the onions are brown, add the turmeric and ground cumin. Cook very briefly—for about 5 seconds.

Pour the seasoned oil into the dal and cook for another 4 to 5 minutes.

Serve with rice or Indian bread and wedges of lemon on the side.

Tasty Dal & Cracked Wheat Medley
(Khichri)

Shimmi Chandra

Editor's note: This dish, transliterated *khichri* or *khichdi,* typically combines rice and lentils. The recipe here offers a variation by using cracked wheat (*dalia*) instead of rice.

Serves 4–6

3 tablespoons vegetable oil
Pinch of hing (asafoetida)
½ teaspoon black mustard seeds
6 curry leaves
1 green chilli, chopped
½ inch piece of finely chopped fresh ginger
½ cup chopped onions
1 cup masoor dal
1 cup cracked wheat (*dalia*)

Pinch each of turmeric, ground coriander, and red chilli powder
1 cup cubed of eggplant, in ½ inch pieces
1 cup chopped broccoli
2 small zucchini, cut into ½-inch slices
3 cups water
Salt to taste
Garnish: Chopped fresh cilantro

Directions are for cooking in a pressure cooker. But you can also cook this dish in a saucepan, allowing more time for the ingredients to cook, and adding more water as necessary.

Heat the oil in a pressure cooker. Add the hing, followed by the mustard seeds, curry leaves, green chilli, and ginger. Fry until the mustard seeds start to pop. Add the onions and stir until translucent.

Add the masoor dal and stir 2 to 3 minutes. Add the dalia, followed by the turmeric, ground coriander, and red chilli powder. Stir and cook for a few minutes.

Stir in the eggplant, broccoli, and zucchini and when well mixed, add 3 cups of water and salt to taste.

Close the lid of the pressure cooker and cook for 5 minutes. (If using a regular saucepan, cook longer, for 10 minutes or more, till the vegetables are done.)

Garnish with cilantro and serve hot with raita or plain yogurt.

Mixed Dal (1)

Jaya Kumar

Serves 4

1 tablespoon each of these dals: chana masoor, moong & toor
2 cups of water
1 small onion, chopped

½ inch piece of fresh ginger, grated
2 cloves garlic, crushed
3 green chillies, sliced
½ teaspoon turmeric
½ teaspoon salt

For the tarka

2 tablespoons vegetable oil or ghee (clarified butter)
½ teaspoon black mustard seeds
½ teaspoon cumin seeds

¼ teaspoon hing (asafoetida)
1 teaspoon urad dal (with skins)
½ teaspoon garam masala

Wash the dals together until the water runs clear. Soak overnight.

Drain the dals and boil in 2 cups of water with the onion, ginger, garlic, green chillies, turmeric, and salt. Simmer until the dals are soft but not mushy. Stir occasionally.

The tarka

Before serving, heat the oil in a small frying pan on medium high heat. Add the black mustard seeds and soon after that the cumin seeds and hing. Add the urad dal and fry quickly before the spices burn. When the mustard seeds start to pop, pour the oil mixture into the cooked dal. Stir in the garam masala.

Mixed Dal (2)

Vidya Tripathy

Serves 8

1 cup whole moth* dal
½ cup kidney beans
½ cup whole urad dal
½ cup black-eyed peas
½ cup whole black
  chana
½ cup chana dal,
  washed (to remove
  skins) and split
1¼ teaspoons salt (or to
  taste)
½ teaspoon hot red

chilli powder
⅛ teaspoon black pep-
  per
1 teaspoon turmeric
1 teaspoon ground cori-
  ander
1 teaspoon ground
  cumin
6 cups warm water (+ 2
  cups water for later)
3 tablespoons oil

*Resembling small kidney beans, this dal is usually translit-
erated as *moth* and pronounced somewhat like *moat*.

For the tarka
1½ medium onion, fine-
  ly chopped
4–5 cloves garlic, finely
  chopped
1–2 inch piece fresh gin-
  ger, grated

1 8-ounce can tomato
  sauce
1 cup finely chopped
  cilantro

Wash all the dals together, and soak in plenty of warm
water for at least 4 hours. Drain the dals and put them in
a 4- to 6-quart pressure cooker. Add the salt, red chilli
powder, black pepper, turmeric, ground coriander, cumin, and 6 cups of warm water.

Mix well and bring to a full boil on medium-high heat,
uncovered. Skim off any foam, then cover. When the
steam starts to come out from the lid, put the weight on

118

the pressure cooker. Reduce the heat to low. Cook for 10 minutes or upon 3 whistles from the cooker.

The tarka

In a separate saucepan, heat the cooking oil for 30 seconds on medium high. Add the onion, garlic, and ginger. Fry for 1 minute and turn the heat to medium-low. Keep frying until the paste starts to brown.

Add the tomato sauce. Bring to a boil, then add 2 cups of warm water and cook, covered, for another 2 minutes. Add the cilantro to the sauce and stir. Pour the sauce into the cooked dal and mix well.

If not using a pressure cooker

Put the dal in saucepan with 8 cups water and bring to a boil on high heat. Reduce the heat and simmer, partially covered, until the dal is fully cooked (soft), adding more water if necessary. Season as above.

Serve with rice.

Simple & Hearty Urad Dal

Munni Rodrigues

Editor's note: Urad dal is a pale cream-colored with a thin black skin. You can buy it with skins or without skins. When skinless, is referred to as "washed."

Serves 4–6

1 cup washed urad dal
1 tablespoon oil
1 teaspoon cumin seeds
1-inch piece of fresh
   ginger, chopped fine
½ teaspoon turmeric

¼ teaspoon hing (asa-
   foetida)
2 cups of water or more
¾ teaspoon salt (or less)
Garnish: Wedges of
   lemon

Wash the dal thoroughly in cold water until the water is clear, and drain. Heat the oil in a large saucepan and put in the cumin seeds; as soon as they sizzle (a few seconds), add the chopped ginger and turmeric. Keep stirring to avoid burning the spices.

Add the dal, and when the moisture evaporates, add the hing. Stir rapidly to keep from burning. Cover with water and add the salt. (In India, one would say the level of the liquid above the dal should measure to one notch of your index finger.) Bring to a boil, cover and simmer until the water is absorbed.

Garnish with wedges of lemon and serve with roti.

Basic Toor Dal

Aradhna Chhajed

Editor's note: Also called *Arhar.* this robust and flavorful dal is also high in protein and very popular both in North and South India.

Serves 6

1 cup toor dal
3–4 cups water
1 teaspoon salt
⅛ teaspoon turmeric
1 tablespoon ghee (clarified butter)
Pinch of hing (asafoetida)

1½ teaspoons cumin seeds
1 green chilli split in two
½ teaspoon red chilli powder
Garnish: Chopped fresh cilantro

Cook the dal in water with salt and turmeric until very soft.

The tarka: Heat the ghee in a separate pan and add the asafoetida, cumin seeds, and green chilli. Fry for a few seconds, then add the red chilli powder. Pour the ghee mixture into the dal and stir.

Garnish with cilantro.

Serve with rice or chapatis.

Variation: Moong dal can be cooked the same way. You can add tomatoes to either dal when you start cooking it.

Toor Dal & Spinach Stew with Coconut
(Keerai Molagootal)

Shyamala Balgopal

Contributor's note: This dish from the Palakaad region of Kerala is unique to the Kerala Iyer community. Since it is not very spicy or oily, it is suitable for all. Toor dal is high in protein, so when cooked with spinach or other vegetables it makes for a balanced meal when served with rice.

Serves 4–6

¾ cup toor dal
1 cup water
¼ teaspoon turmeric

1 pound spinach
  (keerai), chopped
½ teaspoon salt

For the coconut paste
1 teaspoon oil
1 whole red dried chilli
1 teaspoon urad dal
1 tablespoon uncooked
  rice, washed to soften
½ teaspoon cumin seeds

¾ cup grated coconut
  (either pre-packaged
  or grated fresh, using a
  food-processor or a
  hand grater)

For the tarka
1 teaspoon oil
½ teaspoon mustard
  seeds

1 whole red chilli
1 teaspoon urad dal

Wash the dal and put in a pot with 1cup of water and ¼ teaspoon turmeric. Bring to a boil, reduce heat to medium-low; partially cover and simmer, until the dal is soft but not runny.

Cook the spinach separately until it is done and mash it. Add the salt. Set aside.

Make the coconut paste. In a large pot, heat 1 teaspoon of oil on medium heat, and fry the whole red chilli and urad dal until the urad dal turns a deep golden brown and is aromatic; then add the soaked uncooked rice.

Remove from the heat and add ½ teaspoon of cumin seeds. In a blender or food processor, grind this mixture with 1 cup of grated coconut to make a fine paste.

To this paste, add the cooked spinach and grind again for 30 seconds till the spinach gets blended (but not puréed).

Return the paste to the pot and add the toor dal, and cook on medium for 2 to 3 minutes.

The tarka: Heat the oil in a small frying pan on medium-high. When oil is hot add the mustard seeds. When they pop (in a few seconds), add the red chilli and urad dal. Fry till the urad dal turns golden brown. Add the mixture to the molagootal (stew) and boil for 2 more minutes.

Variation: Toor & Mixed Vegetable Molagootal

Molagootal can also be made with mixed vegetables such as raw banana, beans, carrots, peas, potatoes, or pumpkin, but not okra or eggplant. That is, no mushy vegetables!

Follow the same recipe as above, with the following adjustments.

The dal base
½ cup uncooked toor dal
1 cup water
¼ teaspoon turmeric

Coconut paste as above but use ½ cup grated coconut

Tarka ingredients as above.

The vegetable stew

1 small potato
1 6-inch carrot
A handful of green beans
A small piece cabbage or
  cauliflower
A small piece winter
  squash or gourd

⅛ cup frozen peas,
  thawed
½ teaspoon turmeric
Salt to taste
Garnish: 2–3 fresh curry
  leaves

Cook the toor dal and make the coconut paste as described above, but with a smaller quantity of coconut.

Chop the vegetables into ¾-inch pieces. Put them in a pot with the turmeric and salt and enough water to barely cover them. Cook medium-low till done (do not overcook).

Add the coconut paste and the cooked dal to the vegetables and cook for 4 to 5 minutes.

The tarka: Prepare the tarka as instructed on the previous page. Fry and then add to the pot. Garnish with the curry leaves.

Serve either stew with plain white rice.

Tart & Tasty Toor with Vegetables
(Sambar)

Usha Yelamanchili

Editor's note: This South Indian dish is characterized as a soup or a stew. Regardless of categories, it is a deliciously simple dish with loads of flavor.

Serves 4

1 large lemon-sized ball of tamarind*
1 cup toor dal
2 tablespoons oil
½ teaspoon mustard seeds
10–12 small sambar onions (or shallots) or 1 cup sliced onions
2 medium tomatoes, quartered
1 carrot, diced

Salt to taste
Pinch of turmeric
1 tablespoon jaggery or sugar (optional)
1½ tablespoons sambar powder (available at Indian and international groceries)
Garnish: Chopped fresh cilantro

*Dried tamarind is available at Indian and international food and grocery stores.

To make the tamarind extract: Soak a large lemon-sized lump of dried tamarind in 1 cup of water for 2 to 3 hours. Squeeze out the juice and discard the fiber. (For more on tamarind, see p. 21 and glossary.)

Wash the toor dal and cook it with 2 to 3 cups of water until it is soft.

In another pot, heat the oil on medium-high and add the mustard seeds. When the seeds start to pop, add shallots or onions, tomatoes, and carrots, and sauté for 5 minutes.

Mix in the tamarind extract, salt, jaggery/sugar, and turmeric. Cook until the vegetables are tender.

Stir in the cooked dal and sambar powder and cook for an additional 5 minutes.

Garnish with cilantro before serving.

Tip: You can add a variety of vegetables to the pot. Green beans and an Indian vegetable called "drumsticks" are popular choices (**see glossary**).

You can also add a pinch of asafoetida after you fry the mustard seeds.

Kidney Beans in Tomato Gravy
(Rajma)

Indra Aggarwal

Serves 6

2 cups red kidney beans
   or 3 10-ounce cans
   kidney beans*
3 tablespoons oil
1 large onion
2 cloves garlic
1-inch piece of fresh
   ginger
1 teaspoon cumin seeds
3–4 dry or fresh curry
   leaves (optional)
1 large tomato, chopped
   finely

Salt to taste
½ teaspoon black pep-
   per
¼ teaspoon turmeric
Red chilli powder to
   taste
½ teaspoon black car-
   damom, crushed
½-inch piece cinnamon,
   crushed
Garnish: Chopped fresh
   cilantro

*Using canned beans saves much time.

Wash the kidney beans thoroughly and soak in 5 cups of water for 8 to 10 hours. Drain and cook the beans in a pressure cooker. Put enough water to cover the beans and cook for 10 minutes after the cooker starts to whistle. Remove from the heat and open the lid when safe. If using canned beans, drain and rinse the beans and set aside.

Grind the onion, ginger, and garlic to a paste. Heat the oil on medium and fry the paste until brown. Add the cumin seeds and fry. Add curry leaves (if using), while frying the cumin. Add the finely chopped tomato and fry until the pieces soften.

Add the salt, black pepper, turmeric, red chilli powder, crushed cardamom, and cinnamon. Mix and cook for another 2 minutes.

Add the kidney beans and cook on low heat, stirring frequently, until the mixture starts bubbling. Add hot water if needed to increase the gravy, a little at a time.

Garnish with cilantro and serve with Indian bread or rice.

Garbanzos in Thick Gravy
(Chhole)

Rajni Govindjee

Editor's note: Chhole rhymes with *Olay.*

Serves 6

3 tablespoons oil
2 teaspoons cumin seeds
1 large onion, chopped
3–4 tomatoes, chopped
4 cloves garlic, chopped
1-inch piece fresh
  ginger, grated
3 teaspoons ground
  coriander
3 teaspoons ground
  cumin
3 teaspoons Madras
curry powder
3 teaspoons turmeric
2 teaspoons garam ma-
  sala
3 10-ounce cans of gar-
  banzo beans
1 tablespoon tamarind
  paste*
Salt to taste
Garnish: Chopped fresh
  cilantro

*Available from Indian and international food stores.

In a large saucepan, heat the oil on medium and add the cumin seeds. When the seeds sizzle and brown, add the onions and cook until translucent; add the tomatoes and cook until mushy.

Add the garlic, ginger, and the powdered spices (corian-der, cumin, Madras curry powder, turmeric, garam masa-la). Cook on medium heat for approximately 5 minutes.

Drain and rinse the garbanzos and add them to the spice mixture. Cook for approximately 20 minutes. Add the tamarind paste and salt with enough water to make a thick gravy. Cook for another 15 minutes.

Garnish with cilantro leaves. Serve with Indian bread.

Gram Flour & Buttermilk Curry
(Karhi)

Rajni Govindjee

Editor's note: The name of this dish is also transliterated as *kadhi.*

Serves 4

¾ cup gram flour (besan)
3 cups buttermilk
4 cups water
1 teaspoon salt
3 teaspoons ground coriander
1 teaspoon ground cumin
1 teaspoon turmeric
1 teaspoon crushed red pepper
1 tablespoon oil
Pinch of hing (asafoetida)
¼ cup dried fenugreek leaves (kasoori methi)*
1 teaspoon fenugreek seeds (methi)

* See glossary

Mix the gram flour, buttermilk, water, salt, ground coriander, ground cumin, turmeric, and crushed red pepper. Stir well.

Heat the oil in a 3-quart pan on medium; add the hing and the fenugreek seeds and dried leaves and cook for a few seconds until the mix is fragrant.

Pour in the gram flour and buttermilk mixture. Bring to a boil, stirring constantly. Let the sauce simmer on moderate heat for approximately 30 to 40 minutes, stirring frequently. The consistency should be of a thick sauce.

Serve with plain steamed rice.

Garbanzo Burgers

Rashmi Kapoor

Makes 6 burgers

For the burger mix

1 can of garbanzo beans, drained

1 small yellow onion, chopped

1 clove garlic

¼-inch piece fresh ginger

1 green chilli

¼ cup chopped cilantro (green coriander)

Pinch of garam masala

Salt to taste

½ cup plain bread-crumbs

1 tablespoon vegetable oil

For assembling the burger

6 burger buns

Mint-cilantro chutney (see p. 251)

Tomato slices

Cucumber slices

Red onion slices

In a food processor, put the first garbanzos, onion, garlic, ginger, cilantro, and garam masala. Pulse at low speed or grind till coarsely chopped. Put the mixture in a bowl. Add the salt and breadcrumbs and stir to bind the mixture. Form 6 patties.

Heat a shallow frying pan on medium heat. Brush with a little oil and cook the patties till light brown. Flip and cook the other side.

Cut the burger buns in half and heat each half for few seconds on both sides. Spread mint-cilantro chutney on the open face and layer the burger with the rest of the ingredients.

Note: The burgers can be cooked on the grill as well.

Black-Eyed Pea Burgers

Aradhna Chhajed

Serves 6

1 cup black-eyed peas
  (or 2 10-ounce cans)
2 cups water
1 potato, boiled and
  diced
1 red onion, chopped
1 teaspoon fresh ginger,
  grated

1–2 cloves garlic,
  chopped (optional)
1 tablespoon chopped
  cilantro
½ teaspoon green chil-
  lies, sliced (or to taste)
Salt to taste
2–3 tablespoons oil for
  shallow frying

If using dried black-eyed peas, soak overnight in 2 cups water. Drain and cook in 2 cups water until soft and the moisture is absorbed. If using canned peas, drain and rinse.

To the peas, add the boiled potato and the chopped onion, ginger, and garlic (if using), and mash coarsely. Stir in the chopped cilantro, green chillies, and salt. Make 6 burger-sized patties.

Heat the oil on medium-high heat and brown the burgers on both sides.

Serve on buns. Ketchup optional.

Black-Eyed Peas in Spiced Sauce

Aradhna Chhajed

Serves 4–6

1 cup dry black-eyed peas or 2 10-ounce cans black-eyed peas
2 cups of water
Salt to taste (if using canned beans, you may not need to add much salt)
¼ teaspoon turmeric
2 teaspoons oil
1 teaspoon cumin seeds
1 medium onion, chopped
1 teaspoon grated fresh ginger
1 green chilli, chopped
1 large tomato, chopped
Red chilli powder to taste
3–4 curry leaves (optional)
Garnish: Chopped fresh cilantro

If using dry beans, soak in water for a few hours and drain. Cook the beans in two cups of water with salt and turmeric until the beans are soft. (You can also use canned beans drained of their liquid. In this case, you will add the turmeric later and reduce the salt.)

Heat the oil in a saucepan and put in the cumin seeds. When seeds darken slightly, add the onion, ginger, and green chilli. When the onion is golden brown, add the tomato and red chilli powder. (If using canned beans, add the turmeric at this point.) Cook for 5 minutes, then add the beans. Bring the beans to a boil, and simmer for 5 to 7 minutes. Add curry leaves if using. Simmer till the gravy thickens.

Garnish with fresh cilantro and serve with rice.

Variation: You can add spinach to the beans to make a one-pot meal. Let the beans cook for a while before you do so.

Nawabi Soy Granule Curry

Kavitha Reddy

Adapted and reprinted with permission from *The Indian Soy Cookbook* by Kavitha Reddy, American Soybean Association, 2002. (*Nawabi* can be translated as *lordly* or *princely*.) The contributor has provided nutritional information at the end of the recipe.

Serves 4

2 tablespoons refined soy oil
2 onions, chopped finely
½ teaspoon ginger paste
½ teaspoon garlic paste
10 cashew nuts, halved
1 cup soy granules*
2 tablespoons shelled green peas (or frozen peas, thawed)
3 tomatoes, chopped finely

Pinch of turmeric
Red chilli powder to taste
Salt to taste
1 cup water
½ teaspoon garam masala
2 teaspoons powdered coconut
2 tablespoons cilantro, chopped finely

*Available at Indian and international food and grocery stores and also at diet and nutrition stores.

Heat the oil in a pan, and add the chopped onions, ginger paste, and garlic paste. Fry till the onions turn light brown and then add the cashew nuts. When the nuts turn light brown, add the soy granules and peas. Cook, stirring for 2 to 3 minutes.

Add the chopped tomatoes, turmeric, red chilli powder, and salt, and stir for another 3 minutes.

Add a cup of water, bring to a boil, and then simmer, covered on low heat. Cook until the granules and tomatoes become soft.

Add the garam masala, coconut powder, and chopped cilantro. Stir and cook for 2 minutes. Remove from the heat and serve hot with roti (Indian bread).

Nutritional value per serving: Calories 209 kcal; protein14.6 gm; carbohydrate 18.9 gm; fat 10.2 gm.

Tofu in Chilli Sauce

Kavitha Reddy

Adapted and reprinted with permission from *The Indian Soy Cookbook* by Kavitha Reddy, American Soybean Association, 2002. The contributor has provided nutritional information at the end of the recipe.

Serves 4

2 tablespoons corn flour
2 tablespoons refined
  wheat flour
Salt to taste
½ pound of tofu,* cut
  into 1½ inch cubes
4 tablespoons refined
  soy oil for deep frying
Green chillies, chopped,
  to taste

1 onion, chopped finely
1 tablespoon chilli sauce
2 tablespoons tomato
  ketchup
2 teaspoons soy sauce
1 teaspoon fresh ginger,
  grated
Black pepper to taste

*See glossary

Make a thick batter of pouring consistency by combining the corn flour, refined wheat flour, and salt with water. Dip the cubed tofu pieces in the batter to coat. Set aside.

In a deep pan, heat the oil and fry the tofu till light brown in color. Remove from the oil and drain on paper towels. Save 2 tablespoons of oil and discard the rest.

Heat the 2 tablespoons of oil and stir-fry the green chillies and onions for 30 seconds. Add the chilli sauce, ketchup, soy sauce, ginger, ground pepper, and salt as needed. Slide in the tofu pieces, stir well, and remove from the heat.

Serve hot with noodles.

Nutritional value per serving: Calories 228 kcal; protein 5.6 gm; carbohydrate 16.2 gm; fat 15.1 gm.

Easy-Bake Tofu Lasagna

Vijaya Jain

Serves 8

2 teaspoons cooking oil or any vegetable oil in spray

1 pound firm or medium firm tofu,* mashed

1 teaspoon ground coriander

1 teaspoon crushed red peppers

1 cup onions, chopped

2 or 3 cloves fresh garlic chopped (optional)

½ cup grated fresh carrots

1 cup chopped fresh green peppers or mixed red/green peppers

½ cup chopped fresh chopped spinach

2 jars (24 ounces each) of pasta sauce

1 pound no-boil lasagna noodles

4 cups part-skim mozzarella cheese

1 cup water

*See glossary

Preheat oven to 350 degrees F.

Spray or spread a light layer of cooking oil on the bottom and sides of a 9-inch x 13-inch or 10-inch x 15-inch baking pan.

Mix the ground coriander and crushed red peppers into the mashed tofu.

Mix all the fresh chopped vegetables, including the onion and garlic (if using) and set aside.

Cover the bottom of the baking pan with a layer of sauce.

Carefully place one layer of lasagna noodles on top of the sauce. Sprinkle a layer of the spiced tofu mix on top of the sauce. Sprinkle a layer of chopped mixed vegetables over the tofu layer. Sprinkle a thin layer of the cheese over the vegetable layer.

Continue layering noodles, sauce, tofu, vegetables, and cheese, ending with cheese.

Use 1 cup of water to rinse the jars and pour the water around the edge of the baking pan.

Cover with foil and bake at 350 degrees F. for 60 to 75 minutes until the lasagna noodles are soft.

Uncover and bake for another 10 to15 minutes to allow some of the liquid from the sauce to evaporate.

Remove lasagna from the oven and let it cool for 10 minutes before cutting and serving.

Suggestion: This dish can be prepared in advance and frozen for later use.

ℭ
Vegetables

Writer and politician Shashi Tharoor describes India as "an ageless civilization . . . the birthplace of four major religions, a dozen different traditions of classical dance, and three hundred ways of cooking a potato." You will indeed find your share of potato recipes in this collection. Interestingly, in India potatoes are categorized as a vegetable, and serving potatoes does not mean you have taken care of your carbs! In fact, potato dishes are regularly served with bread or rice. But potatoes aside, India is famed for its balanced vegetarian cuisine. Aside from a rich variety in dals, which offer vegetable protein, there are fresh seasonal vegetables. Visiting a vegetable market (*sabzi mandi*) dazzles the eyes. The vibrantly colored vegetables piled high in carts and stalls are sure to seduce the beholder. You may, however, be dismayed to see the same colorful vegetables reduced to muted hues when cooked and served at your table. Keep in mind the loss of color will be compensated for by the explosion of tastes that combine the inherent flavor of the vegetable with a unique mix of spices. What you lose in color you gain in taste. Whether lightly or highly spiced, cooked vegetables are always eaten with rice or bread, which help to buffer the spices. Fresh, chopped cilantro is a popular garnish to brighten the platter. (For a note on cooking specific vegetables **see glossary, Vegetables, cooked.**)

Oven-Roasted Eggplant Slices

Hans Henrich Hock

Serves: 4–6

3 teaspoons ground coriander
½ teaspoon turmeric
1 teaspoon hot paprika
1 teaspoon ground black pepper
½ teaspoon salt
1 medium onion, coarsely chopped
4 "oriental," long, purple eggplants
2½ tablespoons cooking oil
Garnish: Chopped fresh cilantro

Preheat oven to 425 degrees F.

Mix the spices, the chopped onions, and the oil thoroughly in a closeable container.

Trim the ends of the eggplants and slice crosswise into two or three equal parts; cut each part lengthwise into thin slices. Mix the eggplant slices with the onion/spice mixture in the closed container, shaking gently.

Place the coated eggplant slices in a thin layer on a slightly greased cookie sheet. (For this quantity you will need two cookie sheets.) Bake for 15 minutes. Check to see if eggplant is getting done; turn over and bake for another 10 minutes, watching for signs of burning.

Remove when onions are nicely browned and eggplant is cooked. Cook longer for additional crispness.

Broiled Eggplant Purée with Spices
(Baingan ka Bharta)

Pomila Ahuja

Serves 4

1 eggplant
3 tablespoons vegetable
  oil
1 teaspoon cumin seeds
1-inch piece of fresh
  ginger, chopped
1 medium onion, thickly
  chopped

2 medium tomatoes,
  chopped
15–20 sprigs of cilantro,
  including stems,
  chopped
1½ teaspoons salt or to
  taste
2 green chillies (or to
  taste)

Wash and dry the eggplant. Make a few deep gashes in the surface and broil in the oven on high until the eggplant is soft and the skin is burnt. When the eggplant has cooled, peel off the skin. Mash the eggplant and set aside.

Heat the oil in a frying pan on medium heat and fry the cumin seeds till they start to sizzle. Add the ginger and fry till golden brown. Add the onions and fry until tender (about 5 minutes). Stir in the tomatoes and cilantro; then add the salt and chillies.

Cook until the tomatoes soften, then add the eggplant and mix well, stirring frequently.

The bharta* is ready when the liquid has evaporated.

* See glossary

Stuffed Baby Eggplants
(Guthi Vankaya Kura)

Padma Reddy

Contributor's note: This curry from Andhra Pradesh in South India is done in a variety of ways with different combinations of ingredients. This version comes from my grandmother's village in Rayalaseema. I still enjoy it, as much as I enjoyed it the first time I tried it. As a former nutritionist, I have to admit that this is perhaps not the healthiest option, given the ingredients and method of cooking, but it is something one can afford to indulge in every now and then.

Serves 4–6

For the stuffing

1 tablespoon poppy seeds	Salt to taste
1 medium-sized garlic clove, minced	¾ teaspoon red chilli powder
1 cup grated, unsweetened coconut	¼ teaspoon turmeric
	1 tablespoon oil (corn or olive oil)

8–10 baby eggplants (a variety of small eggplants)
2–3 tablespoons oil (corn or olive oil)

Making the stuffing
Grind the poppy seeds into a fine powder. Cut the garlic clove into small pieces. Add the garlic and the remaining stuffing ingredients to the poppy seed powder (except the oil) and grind again, *coarsely*. Adjust salt and red chilli powder to taste. Mix the oil with the ground mixture. The oil will bind the mixture and make it easier for stuffing and cooking.

Preparing the eggplants
Trim the stems of the eggplants so they are ¾ to 1 inch long. Starting at the bottom carefully cut the eggplant vertically in half until you're about ¼-inch from the

142

crown (stem end). Cut each half again so that each eggplant is divided into quarters but is still held together firmly at the crown.

Fill each eggplant generously with the prepared stuffing, taking care not to break the body apart. Make sure the stuffing is contained within the eggplant, and wipe off excess from the outside to keep stuffing from charring while cooking.

Cooking
Heat the oil on medium-low in a frying pan; place the stuffed eggplants gently in the pan. Cover and cook the eggplants till the skin and flesh are tender to touch. Turn the eggplants, taking care not to break them until all sides are cooked and the skin has developed a light crispness.

This dish is best eaten with plain rice or jeera rice (p. 194).

Eggplant & Potato with Cilantro Masala

Sowmya Anand

Serves 4

For the cilantro masala

1 bunch cilantro, finely chopped

1 teaspoon ground cumin

3–4 teaspoons ground coriander

1 teaspoon red chilli powder

1 teaspoon garam masala

1 generous tablespoon gram flour (besan)

1 teaspoon sugar or gur* (optional)

*See glossary

---

3 tablespoons oil

A generous pinch of hing (asafoetida)

1 teaspoon whole cumin seeds

1 large eggplant (any variety) or 4–5 small

eggplants, cut into 1½-inch cubes

2–3 potatoes, peeled and cut into 1½-inch cubes

1 cup water

Salt to taste

Mix the cilantro with the ground cumin, ground coriander, red chilli powder, garam masala, chickpea flour, and sugar/gur (if using).

In a karhai (or wok), heat the oil on medium-high and add the hing and whole cumin seeds, cooking till the seeds turn dark brown.

Reduce the heat to medium and add the cilantro paste. Stir till the masala darkens and turns aromatic and does not smell raw anymore.

Add the eggplant and potatoes and stir until they are more or less evenly coated with the cilantro masala.

Add 1 cup of water (or more depending on how much gravy you want) and salt to taste. Increase the heat to medium-high and bring to a boil. Cover and simmer till the vegetables are completely soft (20 minutes or more if necessary).

Super-Easy Potatoes & Peas
(Alu-Matar)

Tulsi Dharmarajan

Adapted and reprinted with permission from the contributor's blog, http://tulsid.wordpress.com/category/food/.

Serves 4–6

5 medium potatoes
2 tablespoons oil
1 teaspoon whole cumin seeds
2 whole dried red chillies
1 onion, chopped
½ inch fresh ginger, finely chopped
2 cloves garlic, finely chopped
¼ teaspoon turmeric
¼ teaspoon ground cumin
½ teaspoon red chilli powder
1 teaspoon garam masala
Pinch of sugar
Salt to taste
3 tomatoes, chopped
¼ teaspoon gram flour (besan)
3 tablespoons water
½ cup frozen peas, thawed
Garnish: Chopped fresh cilantro

Parboil the potatoes; peel and cut them into ½-inch cubes and keep aside. (This can be done a day ahead of time.)

In a skillet, heat the oil on medium-high. Add the whole cumin seeds and dried red chillies. When the cumin seeds start to brown, add the onion. When the onion turns translucent and starts to brown, add the ginger and garlic.

Cook for about 1 minute and then add the turmeric, ground cumin, red chilli powder, garam masala, a pinch of sugar, and salt. Fry for a few seconds, till the masala is blended and aromatic, stirring constantly.

Add the chopped tomato. Cook fully until the mixture becomes a paste and the oil separates from the solids.

Make a paste with the gram flour and a little water. Add it to the mixture and stir well.

Put in the potatoes with 4 tablespoons of water, cover and cook till they are done, adding more water as needed to cook the potatoes.

Add the frozen peas and cook for another 5 minutes.

Garnish with chopped cilantro.

Spiced Whole Potatoes with Yogurt & Sour Cream
(Dum Alu)

Jaya Kumar

Serves 4

1 pound red potatoes or 1 pound canned potatoes
1 small onion, halved
1 tablespoon vegetable oil
1 tablespoon butter
½ teaspoon cumin seeds
1 green chilli, chopped
1½-inch piece fresh ginger, finely ground
½ teaspoon ground coriander
½ teaspoon red chilli powder
Pinch of garam masala
1 teaspoon salt or to taste
4 tablespoons yogurt
2 tablespoons sour cream

Boil and peel the potatoes. If using canned potatoes, drain and set aside. Chop half the onion, and grind the other half. Keep separate.

Heat the oil and butter on medium heat and add the cumin seeds, stirring frequently. When the cumin seeds sizzle and darken, add the chopped onion and green chilli and fry till the chopped onions are translucent.

Add the potatoes, ground onions, and ginger. Add the ground coriander, red chilli powder, garam masala, and salt. Reduce the heat to low, cover and cook till the potatoes are done. They will cook in their own steam. Fold in the yogurt and sour cream, and coat the potatoes. Cook another 5 minutes.

Hint: This dish will absorb more flavor if cooked the night before and refrigerated.

Quick & Tasty Five-Spice Potatoes
(Panch Phoran Alu)

Usha Jain

Editor's note: "Five-spice" here does not refer to the popular Chinese five-spice combination but to a mix of uniquely Indian whole spices called *panch phoran* frequently used in Indian cooking to lightly season vegetables. Sometimes called *achari alu masala,* this mix consists of the following whole spices: black mustard seeds, black onion seeds, cumin, fennel, fenugreek. **(See glossary)**

Serves 4

2 tablespoons vegetable oil
2½ teaspoons of panch phoran spice mix*
Whole dried red chillies (optional)
Two tomatoes, finely chopped

2½ teaspoons turmeric
Salt to taste
4 potatoes, boiled and peeled
1½ cups water
Garnish: Chopped fresh cilantro

*Available at Indian and international food and grocery stores.

In a karhai (or wok), heat the oil on medium. Add the panch phoran spices. When the spices start to sputter, add the dried red chillies (if using), tomatoes, turmeric, and salt. Fry on medium heat till the tomatoes soften, 8 to 10 minutes.

Break the cooked potatoes into pieces by hand (they are not typically sliced) and mix with the spiced tomatoes. Gently stir in 1½ cups of water, and bring to a boil. Simmer for 15 to 20 minutes.

Garnish with chopped cilantro.

Serve with puris or naan (see *Breads*).

Mashed Potatoes with a Zing
(Alu ka Bharta)

Zarina Hock

Serves 4–6

4–6 medium yellow potatoes

4–6 tablespoons extra-virgin olive oil

2 hot green chillies, chopped (optional)

2 teaspoons ground dry-roasted cumin* or to taste

A handful of cilantro, chopped

1 medium red onion, chopped fine

1 teaspoon red chilli pepper or to taste

Freshly ground black pepper

Salt to taste

2–3 tablespoons fresh lemon juice or to taste

*See p. 20

Boil the potatoes in salted water till they are completely cooked. When cool, peel and mash them coarsely. (They should not be puréed.)

In a bowl, combine the potatoes with the other ingredients and adjust the seasonings to taste. Serve at room temperature.

Serve as an accompaniment to dal and/or a curry. May be used in place of regular mashed potatoes with non-Indian food if you want to perk up your meal.

Spiced "Dry" Potatoes

Rashmi Kapoor

Editor's note: "Dry" is used in Indian cuisine to describe a dish that is cooked without a gravy. **(See glossary)**

Serves 4–6

3 tablespoons oil
1 teaspoon cumin seeds
3 medium potatoes, boiled, peeled, and cubed
1 teaspoon turmeric
2 teaspoons ground coriander
1 teaspoon red chilli powder
1 teaspoon dried mango powder (amchur)
1½ teaspoons salt (or to taste)
Garnish: Chopped fresh cilantro

Heat the oil in a frying pan on medium. Add the cumin seeds. Fry for a few seconds till the seeds turn brown. Add the potatoes and all the spices and salt. Stir for a few minutes over medium heat until the potatoes fry a little. Add more oil if you want crisper potatoes.

Garnish with chopped cilantro.

Hint: Leftovers are great for hot sandwiches (in a sandwich maker) or as stuffing for alu parathas (p. 217).

Simple Potatoes
(Saaday Alu)

Rajni Govindjee

Serves 4

2 tablespoons oil
2–3 dried red chillies (to taste)
½ teaspoon fenugreek seeds
1 teaspoon cumin seeds
4 medium potatoes peeled and cubed

1 teaspoon turmeric
1 teaspoon crushed red pepper
1 teaspoon salt (or to taste)
1 teaspoon garlic paste (optional)

In a skillet, heat the oil on medium and add the dried red chillies, fenugreek, and cumin seeds. When they start to sizzle, add the potatoes and turmeric, crushed red pepper, and salt. Cover and cook on medium heat.

When the potatoes are partially cooked, add the garlic paste (if using) and cook until the potatoes are tender.

Baby Red Potatoes with Dill

Rashmi Kapoor

Serves 4

2–3 tablespoons oil
½ teaspoon cumin seeds
1 pound small red pota-
  toes with skins,
  washed and halved

½ teaspoon red chilli
  powder
¼ teaspoon turmeric
Salt to taste
¼ cup chopped fresh dill

Heat the oil on medium and fry the cumin seeds till they start to brown. Add the potatoes, red chilli powder, turmeric, and salt.

Cover and cook on low for about 20 minutes till the potatoes are done. Add the chopped dill leaves. Stir and cook for few more minutes on low heat.

Variation: You can add chopped carrots after the potatoes and cook as above.

Punjabi Potatoes & Cauliflower

Pradeep Dhillon

Editor's note: This dish can be used to create a filling for bell peppers (p. 167). If you are using it for that purpose, cook the potatoes and cauliflower only three-fourths of the way.

Serves 4–6

- 2 tablespoons olive oil or your preferred cooking medium
- 1 onion, chopped
- ¼ teaspoon turmeric
- 4 cloves garlic, finely chopped
- 1 tablespoon ginger, finely chopped fresh
- 3 medium potatoes, peeled and cut into small cubes
- 1 head cauliflower (1¾ pounds), cut into florets about the same size as the potatoes
- ¼ teaspoon cayenne pepper
- ¼ teaspoon ground cumin
- ¾–1 teaspoon salt
- 1 finely chopped jalapeño pepper
- 2–3 tablespoons coarsely chopped cilantro

Thinly coat the bottom of the pan with the olive oil and set over medium heat. When the oil is hot, add the onion and turmeric. Once the onions have caramelized (brown at the edges, and soft), add the garlic and ginger. Sauté for about a minute.

Add the potatoes, cauliflower, cayenne, cumin, and salt, and mix thoroughly. Cover and cook till the potatoes are tender.

Add the chopped jalapeño and cilantro and toss gently.

Serve hot as a side dish.

Cauliflower & Potatoes

Asha Kukreti

Serves 6

1 small cauliflower
4 red potatoes
2 tablespoons oil
1 small onion, chopped
¼ teaspoon hing (asa-
foetida)
½ teaspoon turmeric
¼ teaspoon red chilli
powder
¾ teaspoon ground
cumin

1 level teaspoon ground
coriander
1 teaspoon garlic,
minced
1 teaspoon fresh ginger,
chopped
1 large tomato, chopped
Salt to taste
¼ teaspoon garam ma-
sala
Black pepper to taste

Wash the cauliflower and cut into florets. Wash and cut the potatoes into small chunks.

In a large skillet, heat the oil on medium-high. Add the chopped onion and fry until it is limp. Add the hing, stir quickly, and add the potatoes. Cook for 5 minutes.

Add the turmeric, stir quickly, and put in the cauliflower. Stir well, and add the red chilli powder, ground cumin and coriander. Keep stirring for 5 to 7 minutes.

Add the minced garlic and stir well till the garlic gives off its aroma, then add the fresh ginger, chopped tomatoes, and salt. Stir for 5 minutes. Add the garam masala and black pepper, and reduce the heat to medium-low and cook covered until the cauliflower and potatoes are cooked. If the liquid from the vegetables has not evaporated, cook uncovered till the liquid dries out.

Serve with Indian bread and dal.

Ginger-Spiced Cauliflower

Hans Henrich Hock

Serves 4

Small cauliflower, cut
   into florets
1 tablespoon cooking oil
⅛ teaspoon black mus-
   tard seeds
⅛ teaspoon cumin seeds
⅛ teaspoon anise seeds
¼ cup onion, thinly
   chopped
½ inch fresh ginger, cut
   into thin julienne
   slices

1 small green chilli, cut
   into thin julienne
   slices
3 fresh curry leaves
¼ teaspoon turmeric
¼ teaspoon ground
   black pepper
¼ teaspoon cayenne
   pepper or hot paprika
Salt to taste

Parboil the cauliflower florets and set aside. Keep the cauliflower water.

Heat the oil on medium and add the mustard, cumin, and anise seeds. Fry briefly till the spices release their aroma. Add the onions and fry till golden brown.

Add the ginger and chilli slices and fry till soft. Watch out for burning. Add the curry leaves and fry briefly.

Add the cauliflower florets and the remaining spices. Mix and fry. If the florets begin to char, add some of the cauliflower water. When the mixture is hot, cover and steam-cook for about five minutes on medium-low or till done.

Cauliflower in Rich Sauce
(Cauliflower Rogan Josh)

Yamuna Kachru

Contributor's note: This is a Kachru family recipe from Purnima Kachru.

Serves 4–6

2 pounds cauliflower
1 cup vegetable oil for frying + 5 tablespoons for cooking
4 cloves
2 bay leaves
2 black cardamom pods, crushed*
Pinch of hing (asafoetida)
2 tablespoons plain yogurt

2 teaspoons hot red chilli powder
¾ cup water
½ teaspoon ginger powder
2 teaspoons fennel seed, ground
Salt to taste
1 teaspoon garam masala

*See glossary

Cut the cauliflower into 2-inch florets. Soak in salted water for 3 to 4 minutes. Rinse and set aside.

Heat one cup of oil for frying in a wok or deep pan and fry cauliflower to golden brown. Drain excess oil.

Heat 5 tablespoons of oil in a separate deep pan over medium heat. Add the cloves, bay leaves, black cardamom pods, and hing, and lower the heat. Fry for a few seconds. Mix the yogurt with the red chilli powder and add to the pan. Cook over medium heat until the oil separates from the yogurt mix, stirring constantly.

Add water and stir. Add the cauliflower, ginger powder, fennel, salt, and garam masala. Cook for ten minutes over low heat, taking care that the gravy does not stick to the bottom of the pan.

Serve hot over rice with cucumber raita (p. 244) and a salad.

Health Tip: If for medical reasons, fried food is to be avoided, it is possible to soften the cauliflower by micro-waving it and sautéing it with very little oil in a nonstick pan. The oil for cooking can also be cut down to 2 table-spoons.

Stir-Fried Cabbage (1)

Usha Gandhi

Serves 4

1 small or ½ large (approx. 1 pound) green cabbage
1 teaspoon oil
½ teaspoon cumin seeds
1 teaspoon finely chopped or grated fresh ginger
1 teaspoon finely minced garlic
1 green chilli, chopped or cut in long strips (use less or remove seeds if you do not want it too hot)
Salt to taste

Chop the cabbage into thin slices and set aside.

In a wok, heat the oil on medium-high heat. Add the cumin seeds and fry for a few seconds. Then add the ginger and fry for a minute, followed by the garlic. Continue frying for a minute or so.

Add the chopped green chilli and cabbage, stir fry for 3 to 4 minutes; add the salt.

Serve immediately. The important thing is for the cabbage to remain crisp, so do not overcook it.

Stir-Fried Cabbage (2)

Shantha Ranga Rao

Editor's note: This traditional recipe from South India offers a seasoning (*tarka*) that can be used with many different vegetables. The dish uses minimal oil, and the vegetables are tasty without losing their crispness or color.

Serves 4

1½ tablespoons canola oil
1½ teaspoons mustard seeds
1 tablespoon urad dal
1 tablespoon chana dal
2–3 whole dried red chillies

¼ teaspoon hing (asafoetida)
1½ pounds cabbage, thinly sliced
¼ teaspoon turmeric
Salt to taste
3 tablespoons grated coconut

In a large skillet, heat the oil on medium-high. Add the mustard seeds, and when they start to sputter, add the urad and chana dal and the whole red chillies. When the dals begin to brown, add the hing. After 3 seconds, add shredded cabbage and the turmeric.

Add the salt and mix well. Cook uncovered till the cabbage is tender but not mushy. Add the grated coconut and mix with the cabbage. Remove from the heat.

Spinach with Potatoes

Tulsi Dharmarajan

Adapted and reprinted with permission from the contributor's blog, http://tulsid.wordpress.com/category/food/.

Serves 4

3 medium potatoes
2 tablespoons oil
1 teaspoon mustard
  seeds
½ small onion, chopped
½ teaspoon fresh ginger,
  finely chopped
3 sliced green chillies
  (optional)
1 small tomato, chopped

1½ pounds fresh spinach, washed, chopped
3 tablespoons dried fenugreek leaves (kasoori methi)*
½ teaspoon turmeric
¼ teaspoon chilli powder to taste
Salt to taste
¼ cup water

*See glossary

Parboil the potatoes, peel and cut into ½-inch cubes.

Heat the oil in a large skillet on medium heat. When hot, add the mustard seeds. When they begin to sputter, add the onions. When the onions are brown, add the ginger, green chillies, if using, potatoes, tomato, spinach, fenugreek leaves, turmeric, red chilli powder, and salt.

Add ¼ cup water, cover, and cook until the spinach wilts and the potatoes are well done.

Note: If the vegetables begin to stick to the pan, sprinkle some water to loosen them, and cover.

Simply Spinach
(Paalak ka Saag)

Vidya Tripathy

Serves 6

2 10-ounce packets frozen, chopped spinach

3 tablespoons vegetable oil

3 cloves garlic, thinly sliced lengthwise

2 tablespoons rice flour

¼–½ cup water

1½ teaspoons salt (or to taste)

2–3 hot green chillies, sliced

Thaw the spinach and squeeze out the excess liquid. Set aside.

Heat the oil in a nonstick pan on medium. Add the sliced garlic. When the garlic starts to become transparent, add the spinach.

Dissolve the rice flour in ¼ cup of water and add to the spinach. Add the salt and green chillies.

Cover and cook for 5 minutes over medium heat, stirring occasionally. Reduce the heat to low and cook covered for another 15 minutes, stirring occasionally. Make sure the spinach does not stick to the bottom of the pan (add a little more water as needed).

Serve hot with rice and karhi or dal. (See p. 130 and also other dal recipes in the section, *Dals, Beans & Other Legumes.*)

Paneer in Spinach Sauce
(Saag Paneer)

Shuchi Agrawal

Editor's note: This mildly spiced delicacy of homemade cheese in spinach sauce is easy to make and nutritious. Adapted and reprinted with permission from www.chezshuchi.com.

Serves 4

1 pound fresh spinach
½ pound paneer*
1 cup water
1¼ teaspoons salt
¼ teaspoon sugar
2 small green chillies, sliced
2 tablespoons butter or ghee (clarified butter)

1 medium onion, chopped
1½-inch piece ginger, finely chopped
1 teaspoon garam masala
2 teaspoons lemon juice
2 tablespoons fresh cream (optional)

*See p. 20

Remove the thick stems from the spinach leaves and wash the leaves thoroughly.

Cut the paneer into 1-inch squares.

Boil 1 cup water in a saucepan with ¼ teaspoon salt and ¼ teaspoon sugar (to maintain the green color of the spinach). Add the spinach leaves and boil for 2 minutes. Remove from the heat, drain the spinach, and let it cool.

Make a coarse paste of the boiled spinach leaves and green chillies.

In a nonstick pan, heat 2 teaspoons butter or ghee and sauté the paneer pieces. Set aside.

In a separate pan, heat the remaining butter or ghee and sauté the onion for 3 to 4 minutes. Add the ginger and sauté for another minute.

Add the spinach paste to the onion and cook for 7 to 8 minutes. Add the garam masala, remaining salt, and lemon juice, and cook for another minute. (If using cream, add it now.)

Finally add the paneer and cook for 2 minutes. Remove from the heat.

Tip: Avoid overcooking, as this will fade the color of the spinach and also diminish the taste.

Punjabi Mustard Greens
(Sarson ka Saag)

Shuchi Agrawal

Contributor's note: This robust dish featuring mustard greens (*sarson ka saag*) comes from the Punjab. It is typically served with Punjabi cornmeal bread (*makke ki roti*) and is usually eaten in cold weather. Adapted and reprinted with permission from www.chezshuchi.com.

Serves 4

1 pound mustard greens (typically 1 bunch)
¾ pounds fresh spinach
1 cup water
1 teaspoon salt
¼ teaspoon sugar
2–4 green chillies, chopped
2 tablespoons ghee (clarified butter) + optionally, 2 tablespoons before serving

1 tablespoon cornmeal
½ teaspoon garam masala
¼ teaspoon ground fenugreek seeds (methi)
1 medium onion, chopped
1-inch piece of fresh ginger, chopped
1 teaspoon lemon juice

Remove the thick stems from the mustard and spinach leaves and wash the leaves and the young, tender stems.

Boil 1 cup water in a pan with ¼ teaspoon salt and ¼ teaspoon sugar (to maintain the green color). Add the mustard leaves and young stems to the hot water and boil till tender (about 5 minutes). Remove the mustard greens and drain. In the same water, boil the spinach leaves till they become soft. Remove, drain, and allow the greens to cool down.

Make a coarse paste of the mustard leaves, spinach leaves, and green chillies. (Do not overgrind).

In a wok, heat 1 tablespoon of ghee on medium. Add the coarse paste of greens and cook for 5 minutes.

Add the cornmeal, remaining salt, garam masala, and ground fenugreek seeds. Mix well and cook for another 10 minutes or so.

In a wok, heat a second tablespoon of ghee on medium, and add the chopped onions and ginger. Fry till the onions turn translucent (about 2 minutes).

Pour the fried onion-ginger seasoning over the greens. Mix well and add the lemon juice.

Heat the remaining ghee, if using, and pour it onto the greens before serving.

These greens are traditionally eaten with Punjabi cornmeal bread, *makke ki roti* (see *Breads*) and jaggery (**see glossary**).

Health Tips
- This dish is often made without onions for those groups in India who avoid onions and garlic in their diet. If you make the dish without the fried onions, it will still be flavorful, and the calorie count will be lower.
- Do not overcook the mustard and spinach, as overcooking will fade the color of the greens and also diminish the taste and nutritional value.
- Instead of ghee, you can substitute vegetable oil, which is lower in saturated fats.

Stuffed Bell Peppers

Pradeep Dhillon

Contributor's note: The filling for the peppers is a Punjabi-style, potato-and-cauliflower dish (*alu-gobhi*), which can also be served separately as a side dish. (See p. 154.)

Serves 4

For the filling
Use the recipe, Punjabi Potatoes & Cauliflower, to make the filling, but the vegetables should not be cooked till soft. (The potatoes should be three-quarters done.) Let the mixture cool before filling the bell peppers.

For the bell pepper cups
6 bell peppers
2 teaspoons of oil or cooking spray

Optional

1 green chilli, sliced
1–2 teaspoons chopped cilantro
3 tablespoons bread crumbs (or more, to taste)

2 tablespoons grated Parmesan cheese (or more, to taste)

Preheat oven to 350 degrees F.

Lightly brush a baking dish with the oil or use a cooking spray.

Wash and cut the bell peppers lengthwise. De-seed and de-vein the peppers to make "cups."

Fill the bell pepper cups with the potato-cauliflower mixture. You may add finely chopped green chillies and cilantro if you like. Place the bell pepper cups on the baking dish.

Sprinkle the individual cups with lightly seasoned breadcrumbs. You can leave out the breadcrumbs, but they add crunch. Finally, sprinkle the cups with grated Parmesan cheese. This is also optional, but cheese gives the dish additional flavor.

Bake the bell peppers for about 30 minutes, or until the cheese starts to turn crisp and brown.

Bell Pepper Korma

Rajeswari Vanka

Serves 6

For the dry masala
4 teaspoons peanuts
3 teaspoons sesame seeds
2–3 cloves

---

1 cup yellow/white dried peas or garbanzos (soaked in water overnight)
½ cup yellow split dal (soaked in water overnight)
5 green bell peppers
3 potatoes
2 tomatoes
6 green chillies
1 onion, roughly chopped
1 bunch of mint
2 teaspoons ginger-garlic paste
½ –1 cup of oil*
1 teaspoon turmeric
Salt to taste
2 teaspoons fresh coconut, grated
1½ teaspoons red chilli powder
Some lemon juice and chopped onions for "finishing"

*Although a half cup of oil will be adequate, the larger quantity enhances flavor.

On a heavy griddle or in a pan over medium heat, separately dry roast the peanuts, sesame seeds, and cloves. Stir constantly. When the spices start darkening and giving off their aroma, remove them quickly and set aside to cool.

Drain the split peas and dal in a colander and set aside.

Cut the green peppers, potatoes, and tomatoes into 1 to 2-inch pieces.

Grind the green chillies, onion, and mint with the ginger-garlic paste.

Pour ½ cup of oil in a frying pan and on medium heat. Add the ground chilli-onion (masala) paste and the cut bell peppers and potatoes. Add the turmeric and salt, and cover the pan. Cook for 10 minutes, stirring occasionally with a spatula to ensure that the mixture is not burning.

Once the vegetables are slightly soft, add the chopped tomatoes and cover again for 5 to 10 minutes.

Place the roasted, peanuts, sesame seeds, cloves, coconut, dried peas/garbanzos, and split dal, in a blender or food processor, with a little water and grind. Mix the red chilli powder into the paste, along with the remaining oil (if using) and add it to the vegetables. Gently mix, cover, and simmer for a few minutes on a low flame.

Before serving, squeeze some fresh lemon juice into the vegetables and sprinkle with chopped onions.

Paneer & Bell Pepper Medley

Asha Kukreti

Serves 4–6

½ pound paneer*
2 tablespoons vegetable oil
1 medium onion, sliced
1 teaspoon fresh minced ginger
1 teaspoon minced garlic
1 tablespoon tomato purée
½ teaspoon turmeric
*See p. 20

1 teaspoon ground coriander
1 teaspoon ground cumin
½ teaspoon red chilli pepper or to taste
½ teaspoon salt or to taste
2 fresh tomatoes, sliced
4 bell peppers in different colors (yellow, orange, red, green), sliced

Cut the paneer into 1-inch cubes. Set aside.

Heat 1 tablespoon of oil on medium and fry the paneer cubes till the pieces turn slightly golden. Set aside.

In another frying pan, heat the remaining oil and fry the sliced onion for a minute or so. When the slices turn limp, add the minced ginger and garlic and fry for another minute.

Stir in the tomato purée and turmeric, coriander, cumin, red chilli pepper, and salt. Cook for 5 minutes. Add the sliced tomatoes and cook 3 to 4 minutes. Add the sliced bell peppers and cook for 5 to 7 minutes, until soft.

Slide the paneer pieces into the vegetable mix and gently stir. Cover and simmer till the oil separates, about 10 minutes.

Okra & Potato Stir-Fry

Tulsi Dharmarajan

Contributor's note: Okra can become slimy when cooked if it comes into contact with water. That is why I start out by cooking the okra and potatoes separately and combining them later. Adapted and reprinted with permission from the contributor's blog, http://tulsid.wordpress.com/category/food/.

Serves 4

20 small okra pods*
2 potatoes, peeled
4 tablespoons oil
1 teaspoon cumin seeds
Salt to taste

1 teaspoon ground coriander
½ teaspoon red chilli powder
¼ teaspoon dried mango powder (amchur)

*See glossary, Vegetables, cooked

Wash and dry the okra before cutting. Cut the ends off both sides of each pod. Cut the potatoes into thin, long pieces (about the same size as the okra).

In each of two separate pans, heat about 1½ tablespoons of oil on medium. Add half a teaspoon of cumin seeds to each pan. When the cumin seeds start sputtering, add the okra to one pan and the potatoes to the other.

Add salt only to the potatoes at this point. When the okra and potatoes are about three-quarters cooked, combine in one pan.

In the other pan, heat the remaining oil on medium and add all the powdered spices (coriander, chilli, and amchur). Add the okra and potatoes back into this pan and stir. Check for salt and add a little if necessary since you did not salt the okra earlier. Cook uncovered, stirring occasionally, until completely tender.

Easy-to-Make Okra

Zarina Hock

Contributor's note: This dish is a great favorite with my family. For me, okra has to be completely cooked to release its full flavor. This means it will lose some of its bright color. But the taste will more than make up for that loss.

Serves 4

1 pound okra,* young & tender
2 tablespoons oil
3 dried red chillies
⅛ teaspoon fenugreek seeds
1 tablespoon red onion, chopped
¾ teaspoon ground cumin
1 teaspoon ground coriander
½ teaspoon turmeric
½ teaspoon red chilli powder
1 teaspoon fresh ground fennel
1 teaspoon dried mango powder (amchur)
Salt to taste

*See glossary, Vegetables, cooked

Wash the okra and dry each piece to keep it from getting slimy. Trim off both ends, and slice in thin rounds. Set aside.

In a wok, heat the oil on medium. Add the whole red chillies and fry till they puff up (in a few seconds). Remove the chillies from the oil and set aside.

In the same pan, add the fenugreek seeds, stir for a few seconds, and add the chopped onion. Sauté the onion till the pieces go limp. Add the ground cumin, ground coriander, turmeric, and red chilli powder. Stir quickly and add the okra. Mix well.

Add back the red chillies, reduce the temperature to medium-low and let the okra cook uncovered for 20 minutes or more, stirring occasionally.

Test a piece for doneness. When tender, add the fennel and stir for 2 minutes. Add the amchur and salt to taste. Cook 2 to 3 more minutes. Remove from the heat.

Okra is best enjoyed with chapatis.

Stuffed Whole Okra

Anupam Agrawal

Serves 4

½ pound okra (small, tender pods)
¼ teaspoon black onion seeds (kalaunji)*
3 tablespoons ground fennel seeds
½ teaspoon turmeric
1 teaspoon red chilli powder
1½ tablespoons ground coriander
¾ teaspoon ground fenugreek seeds
½ teaspoon garam masala
1½ teaspoons dried mango powder (amchur)
¾ teaspoon salt
3–4 tablespoons vegetable oil

*See glossary

Wash the okra and thoroughly pat each pod till dry. Remove the thick stems. Cut a slit vertically down the middle of each pod without separating the two halves.

In a bowl, mix the spices well and combine with 1 tablespoon of oil or 1 tablespoon water.

Lay the okra on a platter. Fill the spice mixture (about 1 teaspoon) into each of the okra pods, taking care not to separate the two halves.

In a wok, heat oil on medium high, place the stuffed okras in a single layer, and fry for couple of minutes. Reduce the heat to medium low, cover and cook until okras are done, stirring occasionally (about 15 to 20 minutes).

Increase the heat to high, fry the okras for a minute, and remove from the heat.

Serve with Indian bread.

Paneer in Tomato Gravy

Munni Rodrigues

Serves 4

1 pound of paneer‡	1 tablespoon ground coriander
2 tablespoons vegetable oil	1 tablespoon cream (optional)
2 medium onions sliced	2 teaspoons dried fenugreek leaves (kasoori methi)*
6 medium tomatoes, boiled & puréed (or canned tomatoes)	Salt to taste
‡See p. 20	*See glossary

Cut the paneer into 1-inch cubes.

In a frying pan, heat the oil on medium-high. When hot, add the sliced onions and brown. Add the tomatoes and ground coriander, and cook till the tomato mixture separates from the oil.

Slide in the paneer cubes into the tomato mixture, and add the cream (if using), dried fenugreek leaves, and salt. Cook gently on medium-low till the paneer turns pale golden. Do not allow the cubes to crumble.

Serve with chapatis.

Health Tip: Traditionally, paneer is fried ahead of time and then cooked with spices, but when you add it at the end, it is still flavorful without the extra frying that adds calories.

Tomato-Rice Fusion Casserole

Sujatha Purkayastha

Contributor's note: This recipe was special to my family when I was growing up in New England where my family had emigrated from India. This recipe evolved as an end-of-summer dish: When it started getting cool, my Mom would take a warm dish to picnics and potlucks. Along with this fusion dish, she would include dishes made from traditional Indian vegetables such as bitter gourd (*karela*) and bottle gourd (*lauki*), if available.

Serves 6–8

3 cups cooked long-grain rice
2 tablespoons butter or oil to coat the baking pan
2 tablespoons oil for frying
1 teaspoon cumin seeds
1 teaspoon mustard seeds
1 teaspoon urad dal, rinsed
1 tablespoon chana dal, rinsed
2–3 whole red chillies
Pinch of hing/asafoetida (optional)
6 curry leaves
2 medium onions, chopped
1–2 cups any fresh garden vegetables (zucchini, green beans, green peas, mushrooms) cut into bite-sized pieces
3–4 medium tomatoes, chopped
Salt to taste
2 cups grated white cheddar and/or Monterey Jack cheese
Bread crumbs (optional)

Keep the cooked rice ready in a separate bowl.

Preheat oven to 375 degrees F.

Select a casserole dish the size of a standard lasagna pan, and generously coat it with the butter or oil. Set aside.

In a large frying pan, heat the oil on medium-high and fry the cumin and mustard seeds, the urad and chana dals, red chillies, and the hing (if using). When the seeds start to brown and you notice their fragrance, add the curry leaves. Add the onions. When these are just golden, add the vegetables and sauté.

Add the tomatoes and salt. Cook till the tomatoes thicken and some of the liquid has dried out.

To the vegetables, add the rice slowly. Stir until the rice is uniformly mixed in.

In the casserole dish, spread a layer of the rice-vegetable mixture and then a layer of cheese as you would for lasagna. Alternate the layers until done, ending with the cheese. Brush with a little butter on top. Sprinkle with bread crumbs, if using.

Bake in the preheated oven for about 30 to 40 minutes or until the casserole is bubbly and the cheese is brown.

Spicy Stewed Tomatoes
(Tomato Gojju)

Usha Yelamanchili

Editor's note: This dish is particularly good when made in the summer with fresh, vine-ripened tomatoes. (For more on gojju, **see glossary.**)

Serves 4–6

4–5 medium tomatoes	1 medium onion, chopped
2 teaspoons oil	Pinch of turmeric
½ teaspoon mustard seeds	1½ teaspoons red chilli powder
¼ teaspoon hing (asafoetida)	Salt to taste
A few curry leaves	1 tablespoon jaggery* or sugar

*See glossary

Chop the tomatoes and set aside.

Heat the oil in a saucepan on medium and add the mustard seeds, hing, and curry leaves. When the mustard seeds begin to sputter, add the onions and fry, stirring occasionally. When the onions turn translucent, add the tomatoes.

Add the turmeric, red chilli powder, salt, and jaggery. Cook till the tomatoes are soft and the mixture becomes thick.

Alternative: Rasam powder can be substituted for red chilli powder to make the dish more spicy. (Available at Indian and international food and grocery stores. For a homemade rasam powder, see p. 226.)

Stewed Vegetable Medley
(Mixed Vegetable Gojju)

Vijaya Jain

Contributor's note: This savory vegetable dish, unique to the cuisine of Karnataka, is typically made without lentils. **See glossary** for more on gojju.

Serves 4

For the seasoning
2–3 teaspoons oil
½ teaspoon mustard seeds
½ teaspoon cumin seeds
½ teaspoon fenugreek seeds
Pinch of hing (asafoetida)
2–3 curry leaves

For the stew
2 bell peppers (or 1 green and 1 red bell pepper), seeded and sliced
1 tomato, diced
Salt to taste
½ teaspoon turmeric
1 teaspoon red chilli powder
2 teaspoons ground coriander
1 teaspoon sambar powder*
1 teaspoon tamarind paste*
Small piece of jaggery* (optional)
2 cups water

*Available at Indian and international groceries. **See glossary.**

Heat the oil in a karhai (or wok) on medium heat and add the ingredients for seasoning in the order listed above. When the spices sputter, add the sliced bell peppers and diced tomatoes. Add salt to taste, and cook, stirring occasionally, till the vegetables become slightly soft (about 5 minutes).

Add the turmeric, chilli powder, ground coriander, and sambar powder, stir and fry for 30 seconds. Add the tamarind paste, jaggery (if using), and water.

Continue to cook on medium heat, until the gravy thickens (about 10 minutes).

Peas & Paneer in Tomato Gravy
(Matar Paneer)

Indra Aggarwal

Serves 4–6

1 pound paneer*
3 tablespoons oil
1 large onion
1-inch piece of fresh
　ginger
2 cloves garlic
1 teaspoon cumin seeds
3–4 dry or fresh curry
　leaves (optional)
1 large tomato, chopped
¼ teaspoon turmeric
½ teaspoon black car-
　damom, crushed
½-inch piece cinnamon,
　crushed
½ teaspoon black pep-
　per
Red chilli powder to
　taste
Salt to taste
1 pound frozen peas,
　thawed
2 cups water
Garnish: Chopped fresh
　Cilantro
*See p. 20

Cut the paneer into ½-inch cubes and brown lightly in 1 tablespoon of oil.

Grind the onion, ginger, and garlic to a paste. Heat the remaining oil on medium and fry the paste until brown. Add the cumin seeds and curry leaves (if using), and fry for another two minutes. Add the finely chopped tomato and fry until the pieces soften.

Add the turmeric, crushed cardamom, crushed cinnamon, black pepper, red chilli powder, and salt. Mix and cook for another 2 minutes.

Add the peas and two cups of water. Cook until the peas are tender.

Slide the pieces of paneer into the sauce and cook for another five minutes.

Garnish with cilantro and serve with Indian bread or rice.

Health Tips

- Since paneer is high in milk fats, you can substitute tofu, which though less flavorful, is lower in saturated fat.

- Another option is to not fry the paneer before you combine it with the sauce.

Mummy's Peas

Zarina Hock

Contributor's note: Every North Indian household must have some version of this recipe. I associate this dish with Christmas week in Lucknow (my family, being Christian, celebrated the Christmas holiday with much entertaining). Winter in Lucknow was the season for fresh, sweet peas. My mother served these peas as a tea-time snack for visitors, along with her famous Christmas cake and other seasonal delights. You can, however, serve this as a side dish with a regular Indian meal.

Serves 4–6

2 tablespoons oil
2 small onions, sliced
1 pound frozen peas, thawed
2 green chillies, sliced (optional)
2–3 tablespoons water
1 tablespoon fresh cilantro, chopped
½ teaspoon ground cumin
½ teaspoon red chilli powder (or less)
½ teaspoon ground black pepper
½ teaspoon salt
2 tablespoons fresh lemon juice (or to taste)

In a wok or frying pan, heat the oil on medium-high and fry the sliced onions until they brown. When the onions start to turn crisp at the edges, add the peas and fry for 2 to 3 minutes. If you are using the green chillies, add them now and fry briefly. Add a little water and cook till the peas are soft.

Add the chopped cilantro and the ground cumin, red chilli pepper, black pepper, and salt. Cook until the moisture is absorbed. Add the lemon juice just before serving.

Option: Add 1 teaspoon of finely chopped fresh ginger after frying the onions.

Green Beans

Rajni Govindjee

Serves 4

2 scant tablespoons olive oil

Pinch of hing (asafoetida)

1 teaspoon cumin seeds

2 teaspoons black mustard seeds

2 teaspoons urad dal

1 teaspoon turmeric

Red chilli pepper to taste

¼ teaspoon salt (or to taste)

1 pound chopped green beans

Heat the oil in a pan on medium heat. When the oil is hot, add the hing, cumin seeds, mustard seeds, and urad dal. When the mustard seeds start to pop, add the turmeric, red chilli pepper, salt, and the beans.

Stir the mixture and cook until the beans are just tender, approximately 10 to 15 minutes on low to medium heat.

Green Beans with Garlic & Almonds

Hans Henrich Hock

Serves 4–6

1 tablespoon cooking oil
4 or 5 dried red chilli peppers
1 tablespoon slivered almonds
1 teaspoon black mustard seeds
½ teaspoon cumin seeds
6 cloves garlic, chopped
¼ teaspoon ground black pepper
¼ teaspoon salt (or to taste)
2 cups frozen green beans (preferably baby whole beans, with tips removed), thawed

In a shallow pan, heat the oil on medium. Add the dried chilli peppers, almonds, mustard seeds, and cumin seeds. When the mustard seeds change color (turning grey), add the garlic and fry till golden. Add the black pepper, salt, and the green beans. Stir and cook for 2 minutes or so. Cover and remove from the heat and let the beans cook in their own steam another 5 minutes or so. (The beans should remain crunchy, so be careful not to overcook.)

Spiced Brussels Sprouts

Vijaya Jain

Serves 6

2 tablespoons urad dal
1 pound fresh brussels
  sprouts, washed and
  cut into halves
2–3 tablespoons vegeta-
  ble oil
½ teaspoon mustard
  seeds
½ teaspoon cumin seeds
¼ cup chopped red on-
  ions

1 teaspoon ground cori-
  ander
½ teaspoon turmeric
½ teaspoon crushed red
  pepper
½ cup chopped toma-
  toes
Salt to taste
1 teaspoon fresh ginger,
  chopped
Garnish: ¼ cup chopped
  fresh cilantro

Dry-roast 2 tablespoons of urad dal on a griddle on medium heat. Allow to cool and then grind to a powder. Set
aside.

Steam the brussels sprouts for 5 minutes. Set aside.

Heat the vegetable oil in a saucepan on medium-high.
Add the mustard and cumin seeds. When the seeds sputter, add the onions and sauté for 2 minutes.

Stir in the ground coriander, turmeric, and crushed red
pepper and immediately add the chopped tomatoes. Add
the brussels sprouts and mix gently. Add salt to taste. Mix
in the chopped ginger and the roasted powdered urad
dal.

Cover and cook on low heat for 3 to 4 minutes. Garnish
with cilantro before serving.

Quick-Cooking Carrots with Fenugreek Leaves
(Gajar-Methi)

Umeeta Sadarangani

Contributor's note: This is my mother's recipe. Like my mother, I cook intuitively, using what I know and adjusting the quantities as I cook. The recipes that I do write down are scribbled in random order, usually while talking on the phone to my mother in India. I tried this recipe recently, recording quantities as precisely as I could—a challenging task for one who cooks by instinct!

Serves 6

- 2 tablespoons dried fenugreek leaves (kasoori methi)*
- 4 tablespoons water
- 2 tablespoons canola oil
- 8 cloves garlic, sliced
- 2 15-ounce cans of diced tomatoes or 4 large fresh tomatoes, chopped
- ½ teaspoon turmeric
- 4 teaspoons ground coriander
- ½ teaspoon red chilli powder
- Salt to taste
- 8 large carrots, peeled and sliced into discs

*See glossary. Available at Indian and international food and grocery stores.

Soak the kasoori methi in a small bowl, in 4 tablespoons water. (A simple way to do this is to place a strainer in a small bowl and add the water. Soak for 15 minutes. When it is time to use the methi, lift out the strainer with the reconstituted leaves.)

Heat the oil in a large but shallow saucepan. Add the garlic and sauté until fragrant. Add the tomatoes, and stir. Add the turmeric, coriander, red chilli powder, and the methi leaves, and stir to mix. Add salt to taste.

Add the carrots. Cover and cook on medium-to-low heat until tender.

Serve with plain yogurt and hot chapatis.

Hint: This is a recipe that can be doubled or halved, and the ingredients simply adjusted proportionately.

Variation: Substitute one thinly sliced cabbage for four carrots. Cook as directed above.

Pasta with Vegetables in Curry Sauce

Shyamala Balgopal

Serves 8

¼ cup olive oil
1 extra-large onion, chopped
6 bell peppers, (2 each red, orange, and yellow), chopped
2 tablespoons Madras curry powder
3 tablespoons fresh basil leaves, chopped (or less if using dried basil)
Salt to taste
½ teaspoon black pepper
½ teaspoon red crushed pepper
¼ cup heavy cream or fat-free half-and-half
1 box of bow-tie pasta
¼ cup grated parmesan cheese
1 teaspoon fresh oregano

It is best to cook this pasta sauce a day or two before serving.

Heat the oil on medium and fry the onion for 2 to 3 minutes. Add the chopped bell peppers and cook 4 to 5 minutes on medium heat. Add the curry powder and basil and cook for 5 minutes. Add the salt, black and red pepper. On the day you plan to serve the dish, heat the sauce and add the cream or fat-free half-and-half.

Boil the pasta, following the directions on the box. Combine the drained pasta with the sauce and sprinkle with parmesan cheese and fresh oregano.

Cracked Wheat & Vegetable Medley

Urmila Chandra

Serves 4

1 tablespoon oil
1 teaspoon cumin seeds
1 medium onion
  chopped finely
1 cup cracked wheat
½ teaspoon salt
½ teaspoon red chilli
  powder

½ teaspoon sugar
Juice of 1 lemon
1 cup mixed peas and
  diced carrots
4 cups water
Garnish: 1 tablespoon
  cilantro, chopped

In a heavy pan, heat the oil on medium and add the cumin seeds. When they start to sizzle and brown, add the onion and fry till light brown.

Add the cracked wheat, salt, red chilli powder, sugar, lemon juice, and peas and carrots. Fry briefly and add the water. Bring to a boil on high. Reduce the heat to low, cover and cook for 20 to 30 minutes, till the water is absorbed.

Serve hot.

ॐ

Rice

Rice is served hot with main meals in India. Rice, bread, and yogurt are considered essential buffers to balance the spiciness of the other dishes. Regions such as Bengal and South India favor rice with every meal. In fact, South Indian meals traditionally end with plain rice and yogurt. In North and Central India, on the other hand, freshly made bread is served with every meal, and plain rice served with certain foods though elaborate rice preparations are essential for special occasions. The ways of preparing rice are legion—from the simple plain rice to the elegant basmati pullao. For the North Indian, the rice must be fluffy rather than clumped. One of my mother's favorite pronouncements was that for properly cooked rice, every grain must be separate. In traditional households, a new housewife might be judged by her ability to make fluffy rice. On the other hand, stickier rice is favored in South India. The fragrance of rice is *laa-javaab* (incomparable), one that can never be captured in pre-cooked instant rice. Strictly vegetarian or cooked with meat; delicately flavored with spices; baked, fried, or steamed, rice never fails to please the palate. It is also used in sublime desserts, but that is another matter. Ah, many are the ways to dress your rice!

Simple & Fragrant Basmati Rice

Zarina Hock

Contributor's note: The delicate fragrance of basmati rice is legendary. You can rarely go wrong with cooking basmati as long as you are careful not to add too much water.

Serves 4

1 cup basmati rice	6 small green cardamom
1 teaspoon oil	pods
3 whole cloves	2⅔ cups of cold water
1 bay leaf	¼–½ teaspoon salt
6 peppercorns	

Rinse the rice in cold water and drain.

In a medium pot, heat the oil on medium. Add the spices and stir. When the clove heads and the cardamom pods begin to puff up, add the rice and gently stir to coat with the oil and spices. Fry for 2 or 3 minutes, stirring very gently so as not to break the grains.

Add the water and increase the heat to high. When the water comes to a full boil, add the salt and stir once or twice. Cover the pot with a fitted lid, reduce the heat to the lowest setting, and let the rice cook for 20 minutes, undisturbed.

Remove the pot from the heat and let it stand covered for 5 minutes. Uncover and gently stir the rice, making sure not to mash the grains. If some of the rice is lumpy, carefully loosen with a fork or the handle of a wooden spoon.

When serving, either leave the whole spices in or remove them. (Their fragrance will intensify if left in.)

Variation: Add ½ cup thawed green peas to the rice when the water comes to a boil. Cook covered as above.

Caramelized Rice

Soli Mistry

Contributor's note: Traditionally served with *dhansak,* the signature dish of the Parsi community. (See p. 88.)

Serves 4–6

2 cups rice

4 tablespoons vegetable oil or melted ghee (clarified butter)

2 onions, finely sliced

4 teaspoons sugar

4 cups of water

2 pieces cinnamon sticks, 2 inches each

6 cloves

1 teaspoon salt

Soak the rice in water in 4 cups water for 30 minutes. Drain and set aside.

In a saucepan, heat the oil or ghee on medium high and fry the onions till brown. Remove the pan from the heat and drain the excess oil.

In a small pan, put the sugar and brown over medium heat till it is very dark brown. Add 1 cup of water and cook a few minutes till the caramelized sugar melts. Set aside.

Return the pan with the fried onions back to the medium heat, drain the water from the rice, and add the rice to the onions. Cook, stirring frequently, for 5 minutes, till the rice is well fried and appears glazed.

Add the caramel water and cook for 4 or 5 minutes, till the rice is well mixed. Add the cinnamon stick, cloves, salt, and 3 cups water. Bring to a boil, then cover, lower heat to the lowest setting, and continue cooking till the water is absorbed and the rice is cooked.

Serve with crisp fried onions sprinkled over the rice.

Cumin Rice
(Jeera Chaawal)

Manisha Bhagwat

Serves 4–6

2 cups basmati rice
4 cups water
4 tablespoons butter or 3 tablespoons olive or canola oil
1 teaspoon cumin seeds (jeera)

1 medium onion thinly sliced lengthwise (optional)
¾ teaspoon salt or to taste
Garnish: 2 tablespoons chopped fresh cilantro

Wash the rice, drain and set aside.

In a saucepan, bring 4 cups of water to a boil and keep hot but do not let it continue to boil so the volume of water is not reduced.

In a heavy pot, heat the butter or oil on medium and add the cumin seeds. When the seeds darken a little, add the sliced onion (if using). Let the onion turn deep brown, but do not let it burn.

Add the rice and sauté for 2 minutes by turning the grains very gently so they do not break. Add the hot water and salt to taste.

Let the rice come to a rapid boil. Reduce the heat to very low, cover and let it simmer for 18 minutes.

Turn the heat off and fluff the rice quickly. Replace the cover.

Before serving the rice, sprinkle with chopped cilantro.

Coconut Rice

Tulsi Dharmarajan

Adapted and reprinted with permission from the contributor's blog, http://tulsid.wordpress.com/category/food/.

Serves 4–6

2 cups rice
1 tablespoon oil
A few peanuts or cashews (whole)
½ teaspoon mustard seeds
Pinch of hing (asafoetida)

¼ teaspoon fenugreek seeds
2 tablespoons chana dal
6 curry leaves
½ cup shredded, desiccated coconut
½ teaspoon salt

Cook the rice and set aside to cool.

In a saucepan, heat the oil on medium. Add a few peanuts or cashews. Fry until light brown, then remove and set aside.

To the pan, add the mustard seeds, hing, fenugreek seeds, chana dal, and curry leaves and stir. When the mustard seeds start sputtering, add the shredded coconut and salt.

Keep stirring until the coconut begins to brown (coconut burns very quickly, so be watchful). Add the rice and gently stir to combine all the ingredients.

Add the nuts before serving.

Lemon Rice

Yamuna Kachru

Serves 4–5 people as a meal and 8–10 as a side dish

1 cup white rice (any variety)

2 tablespoons vegetable oil

¼ cup whole peanuts

¼ cup whole cashews

½ teaspoon black mustard seeds

½ cumin seeds

1 tablespoon chana dal (small, yellow, split chickpeas)

1 tablespoon urad dal

2–3 green chillies, Indian or Thai variety, slit vertically

12–15 fresh curry leaves

½ teaspoon turmeric

Salt to taste (start with ¾ teaspoon and add as needed)

Juice of 2 juicy limes

10–12 sprigs of fresh cilantro, chopped

Cook the rice ahead of time and set aside in a bowl.

In a skillet, heat 1 tablespoon of oil. Add the peanuts and fry them till they turn light brown. Remove and set aside. Fry the cashews next until they are golden brown. Remove and set aside.

In the same skillet, heat another tablespoon of oil. Add the mustard and cumin seeds. When seeds start to sputter, add the chana dal and urad dal. Sauté the dals till they turn golden.

Add the split green chillies and curry leaves. Sprinkle half teaspoon of turmeric (for color). Stir and sauté for a few seconds.

Add the contents of the skillet and also the toasted peanuts and cashews to the cooked rice. Stir in the salt and sprinkle with lime juice. Without breaking the rice grains, combine thoroughly and delicately with a big slotted spoon.

Taste to see if the rice is tangy enough. If not, gently stir in some more lime juice and salt. (The rice will absorb the lime juice, and the tanginess will decrease in intensity after some time.)

Sprinkle the chopped cilantro over the lemon rice.

Serve with raita and pappadam as a meal or as a side dish, along with a full complement of other side dishes.

Spiced Rice with Lentils

Zohreh Sullivan

Serves 4–6

1 cup dried brown lentils (washed)
1 cup basmati rice (washed)
2 teaspoons vegetable oil
1-inch piece of cinnamon stick
2 whole cloves
1 tablespoon cumin seeds
3 garlic cloves, chopped
2 teaspoons chopped fresh ginger
4 cups water
2 teaspoons salt
1 teaspoon sugar
¼ teaspoon turmeric
½ cup chopped fresh cilantro
¼ cup fresh lime juice

Rinse and drain the lentils and rice separately and set aside.

In a large, heavy saucepan, heat the oil over medium-high heat. Add the cinnamon, cloves, and cumin seeds, and sauté about 2 minutes.

Add the garlic and ginger; sauté about 2 minutes. Add the water, salt, sugar, and turmeric and bring to a boil. Boil for a few minutes.

Reduce the heat and add the lentils. Cook for 8 to 10 minutes. Increase the heat to high, add the rice, and boil for 5 minutes.

Reduce the heat, cover, and simmer about 15 minutes longer, until the lentils and rice are tender, and the liquid is absorbed. Let stand covered for 5 minutes.

Mix in chopped cilantro and lime juice.

Vegetable Biryani with Tofu

Vidya Tripathy

Serves 4

1 cup basmati rice
1 cup extra-firm tofu*
Cooking oil spray +3 tablespoons vegetable oil
1 teaspoon ground coriander
1 teaspoon ground cumin
1 teaspoon salt (or to taste)
½ teaspoon turmeric
¼ teaspoon red chilli powder

4–6 small green cardamom pods
5 whole cloves
1 small onion, chopped
2 cloves garlic, finely chopped
½-inch piece fresh ginger, finely chopped
⅓ cup cashew nuts
¼ cup raisins
1 cup cauliflower, cut up into bite-size pieces
½ cup frozen peas, thawed
2⅛ cups water

*See glossary

Wash the rice, drain, and set aside.

Drain the liquid from the tofu and cut it into 1-inch thick cubes.

Spray a nonstick frying pan with cooking oil and heat on medium for 30 seconds. Add the tofu, and sprinkle with a pinch of ground coriander, cumin, a little salt, turmeric, and red chilli powder. Fry until the tofu looks dry (about 6 to 8 minutes) and set aside.

In a saucepan, heat the oil on medium for about a minute. Add the cardamom and cloves. When the cloves start puffing up, add the chopped onion, garlic, and ginger. Fry until the oil starts to separate. Add the remaining coriander, cumin, turmeric, and the red chilli powder. Fry for 30 seconds to 1 minute.

Add the rice and fry for 2 to 3 minutes until it is lightly browned. Stir in the cashews and raisins. Next add the cauliflower and fry for 1 minute. Add the tofu and peas and mix well. Add the water and remaining salt. Bring the mixture to a boil on high heat. Boil for 1 minute, reduce the heat to low, cover, and cook for 10 minutes.

Turn off the heat and allow the pot to sit on the warm burner for an additional 5 to 10 minutes.

Vegetable Pullao

Rajeshwari Pandharipande

Adapted and reprinted with permission from *The International Linguistic Gourmet Cookbook,* 1976, compiled and produced by the Department of Linguistics, University of Illinois at Urbana-Champaign.

Serves 4

1 cup basmati rice
5 good-sized garlic cloves
2-inch piece fresh ginger
6 tablespoons vegetable oil
2 small bay leaves
1 teaspoon salt
1½ cups water
1 teaspoon black mustard seeds
1 medium onion, chopped
½ teaspoon turmeric
4 ounces green beans, chopped
1 small cauliflower, cut into florets
1 teaspoon ground cumin
¼ teaspoon black pepper
8 ounces peas
½ teaspoon ground cinnamon
½ teaspoon red chilli powder (optional)
2 teaspoons dry coconut powder
Garnish: Chopped fresh cilantro

Wash the rice and set aside to drain.

Make a fine paste of the garlic and ginger and set aside.

Heat 2 tablespoons of oil in a large pot for about 6 minutes on medium heat. Add the bay leaves and rice and fry until the rice is golden brown. Add ½ teaspoon salt. Remove from the heat and add 1½ cups water. Stir and put the pot back on the burner. Cover and simmer until the water is nearly evaporated. Remove from the heat, uncover, and let cool.

In a medium-sized skillet, heat 4 tablespoons oil for 6 to 7 minutes, until hot. Add the mustard seeds and fry until they start to pop. Add the chopped onion and fry till the onion is limp. Add the turmeric, stirring. Lower the heat and make sure the turmeric does not burn.

Add the beans and fry until slightly tender. Add the cauliflower and ground cumin. Fry until the cauliflower is tender. Add the black pepper. Mix and stir. Add the peas and ground cinnamon and red chilli powder, if using.

Mix the garlic-ginger paste with the vegetables. Fold in the rice. Fry the mixture, stirring often. *Be sure not to break up the rice grains*. Add coconut powder and the remaining salt. Garnish with cilantro.

Serve hot with a curry and raita.

Vegetable Fried Rice

Yamuna Kachru

Adapted and reprinted with permission from *The International Linguistic Gourmet Cookbook,* 1981, compiled and produced by the Department of Linguistics, University of Illinois at Urbana-Champaign.

Serves 8

For the spice mixture

4 tablespoons coriander seeds
4 tablespoons chana dal
4 tablespoons urad dal
2 tablespoons poppy seeds
6–8 cloves
½ to 1 whole nutmeg, broken into small pieces
¾ cup whole dried red peppers

Dry roast the coriander seeds, chana dal, urad dal, and poppy seeds until the urad dal turns golden brown. Add the remaining spices and roast for 2 more minutes. Remove from the heat and let the spices cool. Grind and store.

Note: The quantities above will yield enough to season four cups of uncooked rice. The following recipe uses only half the quantity. The remainder of the powder can be stored in a jar with a tight lid for up to 6 months.

———

For the vegetable rice

2 cups rice
3–4 tablespoons vegetable oil
½ teaspoon mustard seeds
½ teaspoon cumin seeds
2 cups fresh vegetables,* chopped or 1 10-ounce
package frozen mixed vegetables
¼ teaspoon turmeric
1½ teaspoons salt
3–4 teaspoons prepared spice mixture

*1 small eggplant, 2 carrots, 1 medium potato, ½ cup green beans, ½ cup peas.

Preparing the rice
Cook the rice as you would plain rice and set aside.

In a large skillet or 4-quart pan, heat the oil for 1 minute on medium heat. Add the mustard and cumin seeds and heat until the mustard seeds pop.

Add the vegetables, reduce heat, and stir fry until tender. Add the turmeric, salt, and spice mixture. (Adjust quantity of prepared spice mixture to suit your taste.)

Remove the vegetables from the heat. Gently fold in the cooked rice and mix well.

Basmati & Wild Rice

Zarina Hock

Contributor's note: In our home on the prairie, Thanksgiving is a multiethnic meal. In this dish we blend American Indian wild rice with Indian American basmati for our Thanksgiving dinner!

Serves 8–10

2 cups basmati rice (extra-long grain if possible)
1 cup long-grain wild rice
2 tablespoons olive oil
A few black peppercorns
2 bay leaves
⅓ cup finely chopped red onion
1⅓ cup water

½ teaspoon salt or to taste
1 cup frozen peas, thawed
½ teaspoon black pepper
½ cup of pine nuts or slivered almonds, toasted
Garnish: A few sprigs of fresh cilantro or parsley, chopped

Wash the basmati rice and drain. Set aside.

In a medium pan, cook the wild rice according to the package instructions. Drain and set aside.

In a large pan, heat 1 tablespoon of oil on medium and briefly fry the peppercorns and bay leaves. Add the onions and fry until they get limp and slightly brown.

Add the drained basmati and fry briefly with the onions. Add 1⅓ cup water and salt and bring to a boil. Cover tightly and reduce the heat to very low, and cook for 20 minutes without disturbing. Remove from the heat and let the rice sit, covered, for five minutes. Then gently fluff the rice with a fork.

In a large skillet, heat 1 tablespoon of olive oil and stir in the wild rice. When the rice is well coated, add the green peas and cook lightly. Then stir in the basmati and black pepper, and gently combine the ingredients so the rice grains do not break up.

Before serving, remove the bay leaves and sprinkle the toasted nuts over the rice.

Garnish with chopped cilantro or parsley. (I use very little cilantro because I think it can be overwhelming in large quantities.)

Meat Pullao Cooked in Fragrant Broth
(Yakhni Pullao)

Annie Pawar

Editor's note: This pullao is cooked with a fragrant meat broth called *yakhni* and is made on special occasions.

Serves 6–8

2 pounds meat (lamb or chicken)
3 cups of basmati rice
3 tablespoons oil
2 bay leaves
6 cloves
2 black cardamom pods pods*
10–15 black peppercorns
4 onions, finely chopped

*See glossary

1 tablespoon ginger-garlic paste
1 tablespoon garam masala
8 cups water
Salt to taste
2–3 tablespoons ghee (clarified butter) or vegetable oil
1 teaspoon cumin seeds
3–4 green chillies, sliced lengthwise
1 tablespoon lemon juice

Wash and cut the meat into 1-inch cubes.

Soak the rice for 30 minutes. Drain just before cooking.

To make the yakhni
Heat the oil in a pan. Add the bay leaves, cloves, cardamom, and peppercorns. After the spices begin to sputter, add half the chopped onions and the ginger-garlic paste. Cook till the onions turn pink and the paste is cooked.

Add the garam masala and mix well. Add the meat, and allow it to cook till the meat juices are released. Add 8 cups of water to the meat. Cook covered on medium heat till the meat is tender and the liquid is reduced to approximately 6 cups. Add salt to taste and set aside.

To make the pullao
In a separate pan, heat the ghee on medium. Add the cumin seeds and cook till the seeds sputter. Add the remaining onions along with the sliced green chillies. Add the drained rice when the onions brown.

Remove the meat pieces from the broth, reserving the liquid. Add the meat to the rice. Measure 6 cups of the reserved broth and add to the mixture. Stir in salt to taste.

Add the lemon juice and seal the pan by placing a piece of foil over the top and crimping it securely and then covering it with a fitted lid. Cook on medium for 15 to 20 minutes till the rice is done and all the liquid has evaporated.

Before serving, gently turn the rice to make sure the meat pieces are evenly distributed.

Royal Biryani

Zohreh Sullivan

Editor's note: This elaborate dish, which was part of India's regal Mughal cuisine, has many regional variations. Cities such as Hyderabad in the South and Lucknow in the North both claim to make the finest and most elegant biryani in the land.

Serves 6–8

2 pounds chicken or lamb

3–4 cups rice

15 cups water for parboiling + 1 cup water or stock later

2 tablespoons salt for parboiling + salt to taste for the biryani

3 tablespoons oil

1 raw onion, grated

1 tablespoon crushed garlic

1 tablespoon minced fresh ginger

1 tomato, finely chopped

1 cup chopped cilantro

1 cup fried onion slices (to be used in portions)*

1 tablespoon garam masala

1 teaspoon ground cumin

1 teaspoon turmeric

Red chilli powder to taste

1 teaspoon saffron (crushed with a pinch of sugar and steeped in ½ cup hot water)

1½ cups yogurt

2 limes or lemons

2–3 tablespoons softened butter (or oil)

Garnish: A few sprigs of fresh mint and fresh cilantro

*Prepare the onions ahead of time by frying thinly sliced onions in oil until they turn brown and crisp. Remove and drain on paper towels. You can bottle and store them in the refrigerator.

Preheat oven to 350 degrees F.

Cut the lamb or chicken into 1-inch pieces, trimming the fat. Set aside.

Wash the rice 3 times and drain. In a large stockpot, parboil the rice with at least 15 cups of water and 2 tablespoons of salt for 7 minutes. Remove from the heat and drain. Set aside.

In a frying pan, heat 3 tablespoons oil and sauté the meat for 10 minutes. Mix the meat with the onion, garlic, ginger, tomato, chopped cilantro, half the fried onions, garam masala, ground cumin, turmeric, red chilli powder, half the saffron water, yogurt, lime or lemon juice, and salt.

Layer the pot with the parboiled rice and meat mixture alternately. Sprinkle a portion of the fried onions between each layer; repeat the alternating process, ending with a layer of rice. Pour the remaining saffron over the rice. Dot with 2 to 3 tablespoons butter (or oil).

Pour in 1 cup water or stock, cover, and bake at 350 degrees for 1 hour.

To serve, remove the rice and meat to a platter. Sprinkle with remaining crisp onions, fresh cilantro, and mint leaves.

Note: In North-Indian and Pakistani cuisine, in a practice probably adopted from Iranian cuisine, the rice is placed in a heavy pot on a bed of thin bread or sliced potatoes that lie in half an inch of oil and water. When cooked, a crust forms, called "khurchan" or "bottom of the pot." This crisp delicacy is served separately on a platter.

C3

Breads

Breads or rice are necessary accompaniments to balance the spiciness of the foods in Indian cuisine. Indians do not eat or serve meals without one or the other; and they generally serve both. Indian cuisine covers a wide variety of breads, many unleavened, which typically are made fresh with each meal. The generic name for these in North India is *roti*. You will find a variety of Indian breads described on the web; some are made with whole wheat, others with refined flour, and still others with millet, cornmeal, gram, or other grains. The basic slice-able bread available in the West is inexplicably called "double" roti. But although Wonder Bread may appear exotic to a few in India, you cannot use it like traditional Indian breads to scoop up your morsels. And in flavor it is no match for the many traditional breads so easily available. Among these are *chapatis* (whole-wheat flat breads, similar in appearance to soft tortillas, that puff up when fresh); *puris* (whole-wheat breads, deep fried till they puff up); *naan,* a baked, leavened flat bread popular in Indian restaurants in the West, similar in looks to pita but entirely different in taste; *parathas,* which are layers of flaky dough cooked on a griddle; and countless others. Ideally, all are fresh cooked with a meal. They are labor intensive, but all mouth-watering and equally delicious! We can only offer you a sampling.

Chapati

Rajni Govindjee

Editor's note: For many of us from North India, there is nothing quite as satisfying as chapati—the unleavened whole-wheat bread that is served fresh from the kitchen with every meal. Individually rolled out, this tortilla-like bread puffs up like a balloon when dry roasted. Smeared with butter or just plain, it is used to scoop up your food. Of course, such an accompaniment means that someone has to bring you rotis one at a time while you eat. This is the stuff of dreams, but you can indeed make chapatis ahead of time and keep them warm so that no one has to keep dashing to the kitchen while you eat. (Perhaps you can serve one roti at a time fresh to your special guests.) Readymade chapatis—frozen or otherwise—are available in Indian and international food and grocery stores, but they cannot match those rolled out fresh.

Serves 4– 6

2 cups whole-wheat flour   1⅛ cups water

Mix the water and flour and knead to make the dough. Divide the dough into small balls (approximately 14 balls). With a rolling pin, roll each ball into a flat 4 to 6-inch round. Cook on a hot ungreased griddle for 10 to 20 seconds. Turn the flattened dough over and cook for another 10 to 20 seconds.

If you have a gas stove, put the roti on an open flame until it puffs up. On an electric burner, put a cake rack over the burner and puff the roti on the rack. Or you can gently press the roti on the griddle with a folded towel until it is puffed up (I use a square pot holder dedicated to roti puffing). Repeat the process with each roti.

Serve immediately, or, if serving soon, stack rotis in a cloth napkin with the top folded over, and place in a basket. Otherwise, wrap in foil and keep warm in the oven.

If storing them, the best way to later reheat chapatis is over dry heat, on a griddle (*tava,* see p. 11), one at a time. (You can find chapati containers on the web, ranging from simple plastic to exquisitely crafted metal.)

Naan

Vijaya Jain

Serves 6

1 package yeast
1 cup lukewarm water
3½ cups of all-purpose
   flour*

1 teaspoon salt
1 teaspoon sugar
1 tablespoon vegetable
   oil

Contributor's comment: I use 1½ cups all-purpose flour, 1½ cups chapati flour or whole-wheat flour, and ½ cup defatted soy flour.

Mix the yeast with the warm water and let the mixture sit for five minutes or until the yeast has fully dissolved in the water.

Mix together the flour, salt, and sugar. Make a depression in the center of the flour. Pour the water into the depression and slowly mix until a dough ball has formed.

On a floured surface, knead the dough with big motions, folding the dough over itself. Place the dough in an oiled bowl, cover with a towel, and let rise for 1 to 3 hours (2 hours is usually sufficient). Once the dough has risen, punch it down and divide it into 12 balls.

Roll each ball out into an oval, ¼-inch thick. Heat a skillet on medium-high and cook the ovals one at a time for 2 to 3 minutes on each side. The naan should rise and form brown blisters from its contact with the skillet. Gently press the edges to cook evenly.

Place the naans in a dry towel and keep them covered. Serve hot.

Fluffy Deep-Fried Leavened Bread

(Quick Bhatura)

Urmila Chandra

Editor's note: This fried bread, which originated in the Punjab in North India, is widely popular as an accompaniment to garbanzos in thick gravy (p. 129).

Serves 4–6

2½ cups all-purpose
   flour
½ cup semolina (suji)
1 cup yogurt
½ teaspoon baking
   powder

¼ teaspoon baking soda
A little warm water
1 teaspoon sugar
1 cup oil for deep frying

Mix the flour and semolina and make a depression in the middle of the mixture. Pour the yogurt into the depression. Sprinkle the baking powder and baking soda into the yogurt. Leave for 5 minutes and allow the yogurt to become foamy.

Mix all the dry ingredients slowly by hand into the yogurt to form a dough. Knead the dough with a little warm water till it is soft and smooth. Cover with a damp cloth and leave undisturbed for 10 minutes.

Roll out portions of dough into saucer-sized rounds, using a little oil or dry flour to prevent the dough from sticking.

Heat the oil over medium heat and deep-fry the rounds. Drain and put on a paper towel to drain.

Serve hot.

Puri

Rajni Govindjee

Editor's note: The name of this bread is also transliterated as *poori.*

Serves 2–3

1 cup whole-wheat flour
½ cup (scant) water

Approximately 1 cup oil (or enough for deep frying)

Mix the water and flour to make a stiff dough. Divide the dough into 8 balls. Roll each into 4- to 5-inch diameter discs (puris). (Since the dough is stiff you may not need flour for rolling; just use a little oil and the dough will not stick to the surface or the rolling pin).

In a wok, heat the oil on medium till it is very hot. Carefully put a puri in the oil, fry 10 to 15 seconds, gently pushing the puri down in the oil with a slotted spatula until it puffs up. Turn the puri over and fry another 15 to 20 seconds. Drain and remove from oil. Put on a platter lined with a paper towel to remove excess oil.

Interesting variation: Add ½ teaspoon salt, 1 teaspoon oil, and 1 teaspoon ajwain* seeds to the flour before making the dough. Follow the process above.

*See glossary

Potato-Filled Whole-Wheat Bread
(Alu Paratha)

Shuchi Agrawal

Contributor's note: This potato-stuffed bread is a very popular dish throughout North India. It is a staple for weekend brunches and greatly relished. When I make alu paratha, I get to hear "One more!" all the time. Adapted and reprinted with permission from www.chezshuchi.com.

Makes 10 parathas

For the dough

2 cups whole-wheat flour

Water to make the dough

For the stuffing

5 medium potatoes, boiled

2–3 green chillies, finely chopped

¾ teaspoon salt

½ teaspoon red chilli powder

½ teaspoon chaat masala*

1 tablespoon chopped cilantro

2 tablespoons flour in which to roll the parathas

2–3 tablespoons ghee (clarified butter)/butter/oil to brush on the hot bread

*See glossary. Available at Indian and international food and grocery stores.

Making the dough

Put the flour in a big bowl. Make a soft dough by adding a little water at a time. Cover the dough and leave it for 10 to 15 minutes.

Divide the dough into 9 portions and form these into small balls. (When you roll out the parathas and stuff them, you will trim off enough left-over dough from crimping each to make a tenth paratha.)

Making the stuffing
Peel the potatoes and mash thoroughly.

Mix the chopped green chillies, salt, red chilli powder, chaat masala, and the chopped cilantro with the mashed potatoes.

Making the parathas
Dip a ball of dough into a dusting of dry flour (to prevent stickiness) and roll it into a disc, about 3 inches in diameter. Brush the surface with a little oil and place about 1½ tablespoons of potato stuffing in the center. Bring the edges of the disc together and crimp together to seal shut. The disc resembles a pouch at this point. Remove the extra dough from the top and set aside.

Dust a little dry flour onto a flat surface and gently flatten the pouch, rolling it into a 5- to 6-inch disc.

Heat the griddle on medium, and place the rolled-out paratha on the griddle. Turn it over when you see some brown spots and cook the other side. Brush the top of the paratha with ghee or oil and flip it over. Press down the edges with a ladle. The paratha will puff up. Cook the other side (it takes about 1½ minutes to fry a stuffed paratha).

Repeat the process with all the stuffed "pouches." Any extra dough that you trimmed when crimping can be combined to make the last paratha.

Serve hot, with plain yogurt and Indian pickle. Butter is optional.

Punjabi Cornmeal Bread
(Makke ki Roti)

Shuchi Agrawal

Contributor's note: Makke ki Roti (a variety of Indian bread made out of coarsely ground cornmeal) is rustic Punjabi bread that is typically eaten with mustard greens (p. 165). This combination has become widely popular in India and is served both at roadside stalls as well as at five-star hotels. Adapted and reprinted with permission from www.chezshuchi.com.

Makes 10 rotis

1½ cups cornmeal (*makke ka aata*)
½ teaspoon salt
¾ cups warm water (approximately)

Ghee (clarified butter)/butter to brush the surface of the bread

Mix the cornmeal and salt in a bowl. Make a soft dough by adding warm water a little at a time. The dough will not be as smooth as regular wheat-flour dough. (Cornmeal dough tends to crumble, so to get the right consistency, it is best to knead it with your hands). Cover the dough and leave it for 10 minutes.

Making the individual rotis
Make 10 small balls out of the dough. There are two alternatives for shaping the dough before rolling it out. You can either (1) wet your fingers and flatten the ball between your palms to make a disc, 2½ inches in diameter, or (2) use a rolling pin and roll the balls into discs. If the latter, dust the rolling surface with a little dry flour to prevent stickiness.

Heat the griddle (*tava*) on medium. Place the roti on the griddle and after about 35-40 seconds, turn it over and cook it for 20 to 25 seconds.

The next step will depend on the kind of stove you have.

On an electric stove
Position a wire rack over the burner over medium heat. Place the roti on the rack with a pair of tongs and press it lightly with a clean cloth or an oven mitt. Turn it over and repeat the process. Both sides should be cooked till well done. Repeat the process with all the rotis.

For a gas stove
Hold the roti with a pair of tongs directly over the flame. Cook both sides on a low flame. (This takes about a minute.)

Brush the rotis with butter or ghee.

Tip
It is easier to make small rotis, so instead of using a rolling pin, I shape the roti with my hands. Thus, while one roti is cooking on the griddle I can prepare the next one.

ℂℛ
Soups

Soups have been eaten (or drunk) in India from earliest times, and vegetarian soups are even documented in the Sutra period (800-350 BCE) of Indian history, says researcher K. T. Achaya. In later times, certain specialty soups won renown such as the white stock meat soup of the Bohri Muslim community in Gujarat and the colonial Mulligatawny soup of British India, which grew increasingly spicy to suit Indian tastes. British influence undoubtedly contributed to an interest in soups, but despite this, soups are not traditionally served as a separate course in an Indian meal, as in European and American cuisine. Nor do they carry the same value as "comfort foods" in the West. Dishes such as rasam and some dals can, according to Western criteria, be categorized as soups though they are always served with traditional accompaniments and never as a first course.

Creamy Cauliflower Soup

Vijaya Jain

Serves 4

5 cups freshly chopped cauliflower florets (approx. 1 pound)

2 cups vegetable broth

1 cup unsweetened apple juice

1 cup chopped onions

1 teaspoon chopped fresh ginger

¾ teaspoon freshly ground coriander

½ teaspoon freshly ground dry chilli powder

½ teaspoon turmeric

¼ cup freshly chopped cilantro

Salt to taste

Freshly ground black pepper to taste

Garnish: ¼ cup chopped fresh cilantro

Combine the chopped cauliflower, vegetable broth, apple juice, and chopped onions in a large saucepan and bring to a boil over medium heat. After 5 minutes, add the chopped ginger, ground coriander, red chilli powder, and turmeric, and again bring to a boil.

Cover and simmer for 15 minutes or until the cauliflower is tender.

Cool the mixture slightly for 5 minutes. Blend the mixture in a food processor or blender until smooth. Add the salt and freshly ground black pepper to taste and mix thoroughly.

Garnish with freshly chopped cilantro.

Masoor Dal Soup

Zarina Hock

Contributor's note: This was a comfort food in my family home. My mother referred to fried croutons as "sippets" (British usage, now dated).

Serves 4

For the soup
1 cup masoor dal
6 cloves
12 peppercorns
1-inch piece fresh
   ginger, sliced thick
¾ teaspoon turmeric

¼–½ teaspoon cayenne
   pepper
6 cups water
Salt to taste
Freshly ground black
   pepper
Wedges of lemon

For the sippets
Four slices of any type of bread
Olive oil spray

Making the soup
Wash the dal several times until the water runs clear. Drain and put the dal in a large pot with the water.

Put the cloves and the peppercorns in a piece of cheesecloth or muslin; tie securely and add the bouquet bag to the pot with the sliced ginger, turmeric, and cayenne pepper. Bring to the mixture to a boil on medium heat.

When the liquid comes to a rolling boil, skim the foam from the surface and stir. Add salt to taste. Reduce the heat and simmer, partially covered.

Check from time to time and stir occasionally till it is fully cooked. It should be soft and soupy. You can adjust the consistency by increasing the water and cooking longer.

When done, remove from heat. Remove the ginger pieces. Pick out the bouquet bag and squeeze the juices back into the pot.

Add freshly ground black pepper and salt as needed.

Making the sippets
While the dal is cooking, heat the oven to 400 degrees F.

Toast the bread lightly and cut into one-inch cubes. Spread the cubes in a shallow baking dish, and spray with olive oil. Bake until the sippets become crisp.

Serve in bowls with sippets and lemon wedges on the side.

Substitute: You can use regular croutons instead of sippets.

Alternative: Instead of sippets or croutons, you can substitute cooked organic brown basmati rice. Add a few spoons of warmed rice to each bowl and garnish soup with fresh-chopped scallions and a pinch of ground dry-roasted cumin (p. 20).

"Some Like It Hot" Carrot Soup

Margrith Mistry

Serves 4

6 carrots, peeled and
 sliced
1 small can frozen or-
 ange concentrate*
6 cups vegetable broth

Maggi Masala chilli*
 sauce (a little goes a
 long way!)
Salt to taste (the broth
 may be already salted)
Fresh cilantro, chopped

*The quantities can be adjusted, depending on how strong you want the orange flavor to be and how (spicy) hot you want the soup.

Cook the carrots in the microwave until tender; then pu-rée the slices in a blender together with the orange con-centrate.

Pour purée into a saucepan and add the broth to get the desired consistency. Bring to a slow boil. Now taste and add salt and chilli sauce as needed and salt to taste.

Before serving, sprinkle with chopped fresh cilantro. The green looks beautiful on the orange-colored soup and tastes refreshing.

Option: This soup could be enjoyed cold in the summer.

Zesty Tomato Soup from the South
(Rasam)

Aruna Krishnamani

Contributor's note: The word r*asam* is derived from *rasa,* which in Sanskrit means *juice.* This delightful dish comes from South India and is traditionally served with steamed rice. It can also serve as a hot welcoming drink on a cold day or a perfect comfort food when you're feeling under the weather. The following recipe has been tweaked over a period of time to suit my taste.

Serves 4–6

There are different kinds of rasam (tomato, cumin, and lemon) depending on the dominant flavor. For this recipe, yellow lentils commonly known as *toor* or *arhar* dal (Pigeon Peas in English) provide the base for the soup.

For the rasam powder

2 tablespoons coriander seeds

1 tablespoon cumin seeds

4–5 whole dried red chillies or to taste

1 teaspoon black pepper or to taste

In a heavy frying pan or on a griddle, evenly dry-roast the coriander, cumin, and dried red chillies separately. Grind to a fine powder and mix together with the pepper.

For the rasam

½ cup toor dal

2 cups water

1 ball dried tamarind, size of a key lime

2 tomatoes, diced

Pinch of hing (asafoetida)

2 tablespoons rasam powder

Less than ¼ teaspoon sugar

Salt to taste

A handful chopped cilantro

For the seasoning (tarka)

1 tablespoon ghee (clari-
fied butter) or oil

1 teaspoon mustard
seeds

½ teaspoon cumin seeds

7–8 fresh curry leaves

Boil the toor dal until soft in 2 cups water. Drain the excess water and save it to add later as needed.

Soak the tamarind for 15 minutes in 1½ cups warm water. When the tamarind softens, discard the seeds.

Boil the tamarind pulp and water for about 5 minutes to remove the raw taste of tamarind. Add a little more water if the mixture becomes too thick.

Add the diced tomatoes, hing, rasam powder, sugar, and salt, and cook for about 10 minutes on medium.

Add the boiled dal and the dal water. Use a wooden spoon or churner to blend it well.

Keep the pan on low heat until the dal froths on top. Do not let it boil. Turn off the heat and add the chopped cilantro.

The consistency should be that of a thin soup. As you add the dal water, taste every so often to make sure you are not diluting it too much. You should be able to discern all the spices.

Seasoning

In a small pan, heat the ghee or oil on medium. Add the mustard and cumin seeds. When they stop sputtering, add the curry leaves and stir-fry briefly.

Pour the seasoning over the rasam and cover. Serve hot.

Tip: To reheat, do not bring the soup to a boil. Always heat on low till the soup froths on top.

Curried Butternut Squash Soup

Shyamala Balgopal

Serves 2–4

1 tablespoon butter or olive oil
1 large onion, chopped
1 big butternut squash—peeled, seeded, and chopped (4 cups)
1 teaspoon ground nutmeg
2 teaspoons grated fresh ginger
1–2 teaspoons Madras or other curry powder (adjust to taste)
1 can vegetable broth
1 can regular or light coconut milk
1 cup fat-free half-and-half or light cream
Salt and pepper to taste
Garnish: 2–3 tablespoons chopped fresh cilantro

In a saucepan, heat the butter or oil medium heat and fry the onions. When the onions turn limp, add the chopped butternut squash. Cook till tender (about 10 minutes).

Cool for few minutes. Take half of the cooked squash and purée it; mash the other half well. Put all the squash back in a saucepan on the stove and add the remaining ingredients. Boil the mixture for 5 minutes.

Before serving, garnish with cilantro.

Kerala Pumpkin-Winter Gourd Soup with Rice
(Olan)

Shyamala Balgopal

Contributor's note: Olan, a South Indian version of pumpkin soup, is a typical dish of the Kerala Iyer community.

Serves 6

¼ cup black-eyed peas (or one 10-ounce can)
½ pound of ash gourd (also called winter gourd)*
½ pound of pumpkin
4 green chillies, chopped
1 14-ounce can coconut milk (light or regular)*

2–3 cups of water
Salt to taste (remember, canned beans may already contain salt)
2 tablespoons coconut oil*

*Available at Indian and international food and grocery stores.

If using dried black-eyed peas, soak overnight and then cook in water till soft. If using canned, drain the peas and rinse.

Wash and peel gourd and pumpkin and cut into 2-inch square pieces. Cook in 2 to 3 cups of water, till tender (5 to 10 minutes).

Add the black-eyed peas, green chillies, coconut milk, and salt as needed. Boil for few more minutes. Turn off the heat and add the coconut oil.

When serving, add a small quantity of plain cooked rice to the olan.

Vegetable & Rice Noodle Soup with Peanut Sauce

Shyamala Balgopal

Editor's note: Although this soup has a number of ingredients used in Thai foods, it has all the flavors that would appeal to an Indian palate.

Serves 4–6

For the peanut sauce
2 teaspoons olive oil
1 medium onion, chopped
1-inch piece fresh ginger, grated
2 cloves garlic, minced
¼ cup crunchy peanut butter
1 tablespoon tamari sauce*
Brown sugar to taste
Salt to taste (if needed)
2–3 tablespoons water

*Made from soybeans; akin to soy sauce but not the same thing. Available at Asian and international food and grocery stores.

For the soup
2 tablespoons olive oil
½ cup chopped green onions
½ cup chopped green beans
½ cup peas
½ cup chopped carrots
½ cup zucchini
Cubed tofu, quantity as you desire* (optional)
1 14-ounce can coconut milk
1 tablespoon sambal paste (chilli sauce available at Asian groceries)
5 cups water (approx.)
Salt and pepper
1 cup cooked rice noodles
Garnish: Chopped fresh cilantro

See glossary

Preparing the peanut sauce
Heat the oil and fry the onions, ginger, and garlic till they soften. Add the peanut butter, tamari, brown sugar, and salt and cook for 5 minutes. (If the peanut butter is salted, you may not need more salt.) Add water as needed to make a paste.

Preparing the soup
Heat the oil and fry the green onions, green beans, peas, carrots, and zucchini. If using tofu, add it to the vegetables and fry till lightly browned.

Add the coconut milk, sambal paste, and enough water to make about 5 cups. Add the peanut sauce and simmer for 5 to 10 minutes.

Turn the heat off and add a cup of rice noodles. Garnish with cilantro.

Butter Beans & Chickpea Soup with Wild Rice

Shyamala Balgopal

Serves 6–8

1 box of Uncle Ben's long grain and wild rice soup mixture

3 tablespoons olive or canola oil

1 cup finely chopped onion

1 cup finely chopped carrots

1½ cups finely chopped celery

4 cups vegetable broth

3 tablespoons all-purpose flour

1 10-ounce can butter beans (baby or small beans)

1 10-ounce can chickpeas

1 can diced tomatoes

1 teaspoon basil (fresh if possible)

½ teaspoon oregano

1 teaspoon ground cumin

2 teaspoons grated fresh ginger

2 teaspoons fresh lemon juice

Garnish: Cilantro sprigs

Cook sufficient of the packaged wild rice mix to make one cup. Set aside.

Heat the oil in a saucepan. Sauté the onion, carrots, and celery for a few minutes. Mix the broth with flour and add to the vegetables.

Add the canned beans and chickpeas, tomatoes, the basil, oregano, cumin, and ginger, and cook for 30 minutes. Add the cup of cooked wild rice to the soup and cook for another 10 minutes.

Squeeze in fresh lemon juice just before serving. Garnish with cilantro.

✵

Salads & Raitas

Traditionally, leafy salads with salad dressing are not served with Indian meals. A more likely accompaniment is a platter with cut vegetables such as radish, cucumber, red onion, and tomato gently tossed with lemon and salt and pepper, garnished with green chillies, cilantro, and lemon wedges. Fresh and light side dishes are a must when you eat spicy main meals. These come in the form of lightly sprouted legumes, lightly cooked and seasoned vegetables, and raitas.

Raitas are refreshing and nutritious side dishes that help balance the spiciness of the main meal. They are yogurt-based and rather like a salad and a dip combined. Folded into the yogurt are any of the following: fresh chopped cucumber, onion, tomato, chickpea flour dumplings, boiled potato, spinach, fried okra, etc. Be imaginative and improvise your own variations. Raitas are light in oil or oil-free; they may contain spices such as dry roasted ground cumin, red chilli powder, salt, black pepper, quick fried-and-popped mustard seeds, cumin seeds, and whole dried red chillies. Fresh mint and cilantro are also frequently added. Sometimes other spices might pop up because spices and Indian cuisine are inseparable!

Moong Sprout Salad

Shuchi Agrawal

Contributor's note: Freshly germinated sprouts are a tremendous source of digestive enzymes; they are also rich in amino acids, vitamins, proteins, and other nutrients. Best of all, they can be easily sprouted at home. Adapted and reprinted with permission from www.chezshuchi.com.

Serves 4

½ cup whole moong beans

1 medium cucumber

1 medium tomato

1 boiled potato

1 green chilli

1 small onion, chopped (optional)

¼ teaspoon red chilli powder

1 tablespoon chopped cilantro

1 tablespoon lemon juice

1 teaspoon salt, or to taste

To sprout the moong beans

Clean, wash, and soak the moong beans overnight in two cups of water.

Drain the water from the beans, and keep them in a covered container in a warm place for a day. Moong beans start germinating very quickly, and you will notice small sprouts emerging in a couple of hours. If you want longer sprouts keep them for a longer time period (maybe two days). Wash the beans twice a day to avoid the risk of contamination.

To serve

Wash the cucumber, tomato, and green chillies. Peel the cucumber and the potato, and finely chop all the vegetables.

Mix the sprouted moong with all the vegetables in a bowl, along with the red chilli and cilantro. Add the chopped onion, if using. Add the lemon juice and salt.

Serve chilled or at room temperature.

This crunchy salad can be served for breakfast, with meals, or as an in-between snack.

Tip: For other sprout recipes (non-salads) see Sprouted Moong Beans, p. 110, and Stir-Fried Lentil Sprouts with Fenugreek Leaves, p. 112.

Parsi Basic Salad
(Parsi Kachubar)

Soli Mistry

Contributor's note: This simple salad is always served with the Parsi dish *dhansak* (p. 88). You can add tomatoes, cucumber or other vegetables to the salad as well.

Serves 4

1 onion, thinly sliced
1 clove of garlic, crushed
  in a garlic press
½ inch piece of fresh
  ginger, grated
2 tablespoons cilantro,
  chopped

2 green chillies, finely
  chopped
¼ teaspoon ground
  cumin
Salt to taste
1 cup vinegar

Mix all the ingredients together and toss in vinegar.

Zesty Quinoa Salad

Vijaya Ramachandran

Contributor's note: The ingredients here are often used in making in the savory South Indian dish, *upama* (p. 37).

Serves 4

1 cup of quinoa
2 cups water
2 tablespoons olive oil
½ teaspoon cumin seeds
1 medium onion, chopped fine
1-inch piece of fresh ginger, grated
2 green chillies cut lengthwise
5–6 curry leaves

1 small carrot, finely chopped and steamed
¼ cup green peas, lightly cooked
Salt to taste
Garnish: Chopped cashew nuts or almonds and cilantro

Cook the quinoa in 2 cups water according to package instructions. Stir to fluff. Set aside to cool.

In a pan, heat the olive oil on medium until hot. Add the cumin seeds, and when they brown (in a few seconds), add the onion, ginger, green chillies, and curry leaves. When the onions start to turn translucent, add the carrots and peas.

Add the quinoa to the vegetable mixture with salt, cover and let stand on low heat for a couple of minutes for the flavors to blend.

Garnish with chopped cashews or almonds and cilantro.

Serve warm or at room temperature.

Options: Add olive oil or ghee (clarified butter) at the end to enhance flavor. These are not essential, particularly if you are counting calories.

Other ways to dress up the quinoa salad is to prepare it like lemon rice (see p. 196), or to use saffron or Italian seasonings such as garlic, basil, and oregano.

To make the dish look festive, add a pinch of turmeric to the spice mix (saffron does the same thing but adds a very different aroma).

Mixed Bean Salad

Kavitha Reddy

Adapted and reprinted with permission from *The Indian Soy Cookbook* by Kavitha Reddy, American Soybean Association, 2002. The contributor has provided nutritional information at the end of the recipe.

Serves 4

4 tablespoons soybeans, whole

4 tablespoons red kidney beans

4 tablespoons green chickpeas (green chana), whole

4 tablespoons chickpeas, whole

2 tomatoes, chopped

1 onion, chopped

1 teaspoon chaat masala*

Garnish: 1 tablespoon chopped fresh cilantro

*Available at Indian and international food and grocery stores. **See glossary.**

For the dressing

1 tablespoon olive oil

1 tablespoon lemon juice

Black pepper to taste

Salt to taste

Soak soybeans, kidney beans, and chickpeas overnight and boil (or pressure cook) until soft. Add the chopped tomatoes and onion to the cooked beans.

In a small bottle with a cap, place the olive oil, lemon juice, black pepper, and salt. Tighten the lid and shake the dressing vigorously and pour over the beans and toss.

Sprinkle the chaat masala over the salad. Garnish with chopped cilantro and serve.

Nutritional value per serving: Calories 221 kcal; protein 14.4 gm; carbohydrate 30.6 gm; fat 3.5 gm.

Garbanzo Salad

Tulsi Dharmarajan

Adapted and reprinted with permission from the contributor's blog, http://tulsid.wordpress.com/category/food/.

Serves 4

- 1 28-ounce can of garbanzo beans
- 1 onion, chopped
- 1 tomato, chopped
- 1 mango with seed removed, peeled, and diced
- 1 green chilli, finely chopped
- 1 large bunch of cilantro, chopped
- 1 yellow or green bell pepper, diced
- 2 limes, juiced
- Salt to taste
- 1–2 teaspoons chaat masala*
- Tamarind sauce to taste‡

*See glossary

‡Available at Indian and international food and grocery stores, this sweet-sour tamarind sauce (also called "chutney") is a mix of tamarind paste, jaggery (raw sugar), ground cumin, chilli powder, salt, and other spices.

Rinse and drain the garbanzo beans.

Mix all the ingredients together. Serve chilled or at room temperature.

Black Bean Salad with Roasted Cumin

Zarina Hock

Contributor's note: This dish can function as a complete meal for a summer lunch since it contains all the essential foods and fiber, as well, when you keep the potato skins. If served on a large leaf of lettuce, you even get your leafy vegetables in.

Serves 4

12 tiny red potatoes or 3–4 regular red potatoes
2 tablespoons extra-virgin olive oil
Salt to taste
½ teaspoon black pepper
2 teaspoons dry-roasted ground cumin*
½ teaspoon red chilli powder or to taste
1 tablespoon lemon juice or to taste
½ cup edamame beans, thawed
½ cup frozen green beans, thawed
1 15-ounce can black beans
1 green chilli pepper sliced (optional)
¼ cup red onion, chopped
1 teaspoon chopped fresh cilantro (more if you prefer)
¼ cup freshly toasted pine nuts
Garnish: 2–3 sprigs cilantro

*For preparing dry-roasted ground cumin, see p. 20. This powdered spice is a key ingredient in the salad, but use sparingly.

Boil the potatoes in their skins and chill them (they should be cooked through but firm). If using tiny potatoes, leave them whole in their skins. If using medium or large red potatoes, slice them when cold (keeping the skins if possible).

In small bowl, stir together 2 teaspoons olive oil, a little salt, black pepper, ¼ teaspoon roasted cumin powder, ¼ teaspoon red chilli powder, and 1 teaspoon lemon juice.

Pour this over the potatoes. Mix gently to coat and set aside.

Cook the edamame and green beans lightly. Do not over-cook—they should be crunchy.

Drain the black beans till the water runs clear. In a large bowl, mix the remaining olive oil, salt (if black beans are unsalted), dry-roasted cumin, red chilli powder, and lemon juice. Add the sliced green chilli, if using, and the chopped red onion and cilantro, and stir.

Add the black beans, green beans, and edamame, and toss gently. Add the potatoes and mix carefully so they do not crumble.

Chill the salad. Before serving, sprinkle with toasted pine nuts. Garnish with sprigs of cilantro and sliced tomatoes.

Carrot Salad

Tulsi Dharmarajan

Contributor's note: This salad is served almost daily at my grandparents' home in India. Somehow it tastes far better there than when I make it! Adapted and reprinted with permission from the contributor's blog, http://tulsid.wordpress.com/category/food/.

Serves 4

4 large carrots, thickly grated

Juice of ½ lime
Salt to taste

Seasoning

2 teaspoons vegetable oil
1 whole dry red chilli
½ teaspoon mustard seeds

A few fenugreek seeds
Pinch of hing (asafoetida)
A few curry leaves

Heat the oil in a frying pan. When the oil is hot, add all the seasoning ingredients. When the mustard seeds start sputtering, remove the pan from the heat and pour the seasoned oil over the grated carrots. Gently mix.

Squeeze the lime juice over the carrots, add salt to taste, and the dish is ready to serve!

Cucumber Raita (Basic)

Manisha Bhagwat

Editor's note: Probably the most popular of raitas, this dish has many variations. It is so common as to require no formal recipe in any Indian household.

Serves 6

2½ cups plain yogurt
1 cup finely chopped
  cucumber
2–3 finely chopped scal-
  lions or shallots
1–2 finely chopped
  green chillies

Salt and pepper
1 teaspoon dry-roasted
  ground cumin*
¼ teaspoon cayenne
  pepper (optional)

*See p. 20

Beat the yogurt till it is smooth and stir in the cucumber, scallions/shallots, green chillies, salt, and pepper. Pour into a bowl and chill or set aside at room temperature.

Just before serving, sprinkle the dry-roasted ground cumin on the raita. (You can also sprinkle a little cayenne pepper on top.)

Hint: If making much ahead of time, add the cucumber just before serving. This will keep the raita from becoming too watery. You can also grate the cucumber and squeeze it thoroughly before adding it to the yogurt.

Cucumber, Onion, Spinach & Tomato Raita

Rajeswari Vanka

Serves 4–6

2 cups plain yogurt
1 10-ounce packet frozen chopped spinach, thawed
1 small red onion, finely chopped
1 medium tomato, finely chopped
½ cup finely chopped cucumber
2 green chillies, finely chopped
1 tablespoon chopped cilantro

Salt to taste
⅛ teaspoon turmeric
¼ teaspoon hing (asafoetida)
Garnish:
½ teaspoon cumin seeds, roasted and coarsely ground
¼ teaspoon dry red chillies roasted and broken into small pieces

Beat the yogurt until it is smooth.

Drain the excess liquid from the spinach. Mix all the ingredients with the yogurt except the garnish. Chill.

Before serving, sprinkle the raita with the dry-roasted ground cumin seeds and the red chillies.

Okra Raita
(Vendakkai Thayir Pachadi)

Shyamala Balgopal

Serves 4

½ cup okra
2–3 green chillies, finely
   chopped
1 tablespoon oil
½ teaspoon mustard
   seeds

1 whole dry red chilli
½ teaspoon urad dal
1 cup yogurt
Salt to taste
Garnish: Curry leaves or
   chopped fresh cilantro

Wash the okra, pat completely dry, trim both ends, and chop finely.

Heat the oil and add the mustard seeds and red chilli. Once the mustard seeds start to sputter, add the urad dal. When the dal turns light brown, add the okra and green chillies (to taste). Fry till the okra pieces get crisp and golden brown.

Add salt to taste. Remove the pan from the stove and allow the okra to cool. Add the yogurt and a little water and stir.

Garnish with curry leaves or fresh cilantro.

Suggestion: Goes well with a dal-and-vegetable dish such as Keerai Molagootal, p. 122.

Spinach Raita
Anju Seth

Serves 12

1 pound fresh spinach
1 tablespoon vegetable oil or ghee (clarified butter)
3 teaspoons black mustard seeds
3 teaspoons whole cumin seeds
3 teaspoons ground cumin
1 teaspoon salt, or to taste
Pinch of red chilli powder
6 cups yogurt

Wash the spinach well and remove any tough stalks. Tear the leaves into pieces and put into a saucepan with moisture on the leaves or add 1 tablespoon water. Cover and steam on low heat until the spinach is tender. Drain and chop finely.

In a small saucepan, heat the oil on medium heat and add the mustard seeds. When they start to pop, add the cumin seeds and ground cumin, and continue to fry. Do not let the spices burn. Remove from the heat, stir in the salt and red chilli powder and allow the mixture to cool. Mix in the yogurt, and then stir this mixture into the spinach.

Garnish with sprinkles of red chilli powder.

Serve cold or at room temperature.

Eggplant Raita

Usha Gandhi

Serves 4

2–3 eggplants, the long
  variety
2 teaspoons oil
3–4 cups plain yogurt
¼ teaspoon salt
3–4 cloves garlic,
  crushed or chopped
  fine

½ teaspoon ground
  cumin (preferably
  freshly roasted)
¼ teaspoon red chilli
  powder

Cut the eggplants into thin rounds. Heat the oil in a skillet and fry the rounds in a single layer on medium heat, turning them over so both sides get done and somewhat crispy. Just at the end of the frying process, add the crushed or chopped garlic.

Beat the yogurt till it is smooth, and add salt. Add the sliced eggplant on top of the yogurt just before serving. Sprinkle with ground cumin and chilli pepper.

Note: The eggplant can be deep fried, but for those who wish to avoid fried foods, using just a little oil is an option even though the frying might take longer.

Chutneys & Pickles

As if Indian food isn't spicy enough, chutneys and pickles are added to further enhance a meal. These are sometimes classified as relishes. Distinguishing between a pickle and a chutney is almost intuitive. Some think it could simply be a matter of texture, chutneys being smoother and more sauce-like and pickles chunkier. Simple chutneys can be made fresh, often in conjunction with a meal. Pickles require a longer cooking and processing period. Keep in mind, too, that the concept of pickles in India is entirely different from that of pickles in the West. For one thing, pickles are not made from cucumbers. Various vegetables and fruit are pickled. They may or may not have a vinegar base and are frequently cooked in oil. Made to survive in intensely hot weather, Indian pickles are packed with spices that serve as preservatives, and they surely pack a punch. Pickles that are sun-cooked in India present a challenge in cold climates. You may wish to pick these up at a grocery store. But chutneys are often cooked on the stovetop.

Cilantro Chutney

Aradhna Chhajed

Contributor's note: This condiment goes well with snacks such as pakoras and samosas (See recipes, pages 30 and 32). The chutney even tastes good in sandwiches!

Makes about 1 cup

1 bunch cilantro
4–5 hot green chillies
Juice of 1½ limes
½ teaspoon cumin seeds

Pinch of hing
2 tablespoons fresh
   grated coconut
Salt to taste

Wash the cilantro and remove the thick stems. Wash the chillies and remove the stems. Combine all the ingredients and grind (in a blender or food processor) to a smooth paste.

Mint-Cilantro Chutney

Rashmi Kapoor

Makes about 1 cup

1 cup fresh cilantro
leaves
¼ cup fresh mint leaves
1 or 2 green chillies
½ inch piece of fresh
ginger

1 roma tomato
4 teaspoons fresh lime
juice
¼ teaspoon cumin seeds
Salt to taste

Place all the ingredients in a blender or food processor and grind to a fine paste with the lime juice. Bottle and refrigerate. The chutney will keep for a week or two.

Serving suggestion: Use as an accompaniment to samosas and other savory snacks. May be used as a spread with veggie burgers.

Edamame Chutney
(Green Soybean Chutney)

Nandini Pai

Makes about 1 cup

2 tablespoons olive oil or other oil
1 teaspoon mustard seeds
1 teaspoon cumin seeds
1 teaspoon urad dal
1 teaspoon chana dal
2 dry red chillies
⅛ teaspoon hing (asafoetida)
1 teaspoon turmeric
¼ cup roasted shelled peanuts
6–8 curry leaves (optional)
5–6 sprigs of cilantro, chopped
1 packet frozen edamame beans (green soybeans) thawed
1–2 green chillies, sliced
1 small carrot, finely grated
½–1 teaspoon salt
1 tablespoon lemon juice

Heat the oil in a frying pan on medium. Add the mustard and cumin seeds. Fry until the mustard seeds pop and then stir in the dals and red chillies. Fry till the dals are golden brown.

Add the hing, turmeric, peanuts, curry leaves (if using), and cilantro. Increase the heat to high and add the edamame beans, green chillies, and carrot. Add the salt and lemon juice and mix. Cover and leave on high heat for 1 to 2 minutes.

Let the chutney cool for 10 minutes; then grind coarsely in a food processor. Add water as needed if you want a thinner chutney.

Variation: Substitute frozen lima beans or use just grated carrots (5 medium) to make carrot chutney.

Fruit Chutney

Usha Jain

Makes about 1 cup

1 bunch cilantro leaves
½ bunch mint leaves
1 tablespoon ground
  coriander
2 tablespoons dried
  mango powder (am-
  chur)
½ tablespoon ground
  red pepper

½ raw (unripe) mango,
  peeled and sliced
15 seedless green
  grapes
½ green apple, peeled
  and sliced
Salt to taste
½ cup lemon juice

Put all the ingredients in a blender or food processor and grind. Add water to make a thick consistency.

Serve as a relish. Refrigerate the extra chutney. It will keep for a couple of weeks.

Apricot Chutney

Ania Loomba

Makes about 1½ cups

1 pound dried apricots
10 large cloves garlic,
  peeled and coarsely
  chopped
1 x 3-inch piece fresh
  ginger, chopped
1¼ cups good red wine
  vinegar

2 cups sugar
¼ teaspoon salt (or
  more to taste)
⅛–¾ teaspoon cayenne
  pepper
¾ cup golden raisins
½ cup currants

Put the apricots in a bowl, and cover with 4 cups of hot water. Soak for 1 hour.

In a blender or food processor, grind the garlic and ginger with ¼ cup vinegar till smooth.

Transfer the apricots and the soaking liquid to a heavy non-reactive pot. Add the garlic-ginger mix and remaining vinegar, sugar, salt, cayenne. Bring to a boil. Simmer, stirring frequently for 45 minutes.

Add the raisins and currants, and cook, continually stirring, for another ½ hour or until the chutney takes on a thick, glazed sheen.

Cool thoroughly before bottling. Keep refrigerated.

Tip: You can add more garlic/pepper/salt for a more piquant chutney and adjust all the proportions to taste.

Green Tomato Chutney (1)

Tulsi Dharmarajan

Adapted and reprinted with permission from the contributor's blog, http://tulsid.wordpress.com/category/food/.

Makes about 1 cup

For the paste
2 green tomatoes
1 tablespoon coriander
  seeds
½ teaspoon cumin seeds
1 green chilli

1 clove garlic
½ tablespoon peanuts
½ teaspoon sesame
  seeds

For the seasoning
1 tablespoon oil
¼ teaspoon mustard
  seeds

¼ teaspoon cumin seeds
2 dry red chillies

In a blender or food processor, grind together all of the paste ingredients.

In a skillet, heat the oil on medium and add the mustard seeds, cumin seeds, and red chillies. When the mustard seeds start to pop, add the paste. Stir to combine and cook until all the liquid has evaporated.

Cool and serve as a relish.

Green Tomato Chutney (2)

Pram Singh

Makes 6–8 cups

2 pounds firm green to-
matoes
1 pound brown sugar
12 ounces malt vinegar
15 cloves garlic
½ ounce fresh ginger
root

1–2 teaspoons garam
masala
1–2 teaspoons red chilli
powder*
1–2 teaspoons caraway
seeds
1 tablespoon salt

*Or more for seasoned taste buds!

Rinse, dry, and cut the tomatoes into small pieces. Peel and mince the garlic. Scrape off the ginger skin and mince the ginger.

Place the tomatoes in a heavy-bottomed, non-reactive saucepan. Add the sugar, vinegar, and remaining ingredients and cook on medium heat for 50 to 55 minutes. Stir frequently and crush the tomatoes slightly after they become soft.

Remove from the heat, and cool thoroughly before pouring into jars. Store in the refrigerator.

Tomato-Onion Chutney

Shuchi Agrawal

Contributor's note: This is a kind of South Indian chutney. Adapted and reprinted with permission from www.chez shuchi.com.

Makes about 1½ cups

2 teaspoons ghee (clarified butter) or oil
¾ teaspoon mustard seeds
6–8 curry leaves
1–2 dry red chillies
*See glossary

1 teaspoon chana dal
1 teaspoon urad dal
1 big onion, chopped
1 big tomato, chopped
½ teaspoon salt
¼ teaspoon jaggery*

Heat the ghee or oil in a pan on medium high. Add the mustard seeds and when they sizzle and pop (in a few seconds), add the curry leaves, dry red chillies, chana and urad dals, and fry for 15 seconds.

Add the onions and fry until translucent. Add the tomatoes and fry for 5 minutes on medium heat. Add the salt and jaggery. Mix well and allow the mixture to cool.

In a blender, grind the fried tomato-onion mix. Add a little water if needed to make a paste.

The chutney is ready to serve.

Coconut Chutney

Shyamala Balgopal

Makes about 1 cup

2 tablespoons roasted black chana dal
1 cup water
1 cup grated coconut
1 green chilli (or more to taste)

2 tablespoons vegetable oil
1 teaspoon mustard seeds
2 dry whole red chillies
2–3 curry leaves
Salt to taste

Soak the dal in 1 cup of water for 2 hours. Drain before combining with the other ingredients.

In a blender or food processor, combine the drained chana dal, coconut. and the green chillies to make a textured (not creamy) paste.

The seasoning (tarka)
In a small skillet, heat the oil on medium-high and add the mustard seeds, dry red chillies, and curry leaves. When the seeds sputter, pour the oil with the mustard seeds into the coconut mix. Stir to blend. Add the salt.

You can prepare the chutney ahead of time and refrigerate. In that case, do the tarka about half an hour before serving.

Tamarind Chutney

Annie Pawar

Editor's note: Tamarind chutney, with its sweet-sour piquancy, goes well with many snack foods, especially pakoras and samosas (see pages 30 and 32). Most Indian and international food and grocery stores carry a choice of tamarind chutneys, but the flavor of fresh tamarind is much more intense.

Makes 1 cup

1 small lump of dried tamarind (½ cup)
1 cup warm water + 2 cups cold water
1 cup grated jaggery*
½ teaspoon red chilli powder

½ teaspoon dry-roasted ground cumin seeds
½ teaspoon garam masala (optional)
Regular salt and a little black salt* to taste
*See glossary

Soak the tamarind in 1 cup of warm water for at least 2 hours to soften it. Remove the seeds and squeeze the tamarind pulp in your fist over a bowl so the juices separate from the fiber and accumulate in the bowl. Strain 2 cups of water through the fiber into the bowl. Discard the fiber. (See also p. 21.)

To the tamarind liquid, add the jaggery, red chilli powder, ground cumin, garam masala (if using), regular salt, and a little black salt to taste.

Boil this mixture till the jaggery is dissolved and the mixture thickens.

The chutney is ready to serve.

Variation: You can add finely chopped raisins and/or dates and cook them along with the spices.

Sweet-and-Sour Lime Pickle

Rajeshwari Pandharipande

Contributor's note: This pickle matures best in dry, sunny weather (a rare ingredient in Central Illinois!).

Makes enough for a quart jar (approximately)

15 good-size limes   ¼ cup salt
1 cup sugar   ½ cup red chilli powder

Cut the limes into 8 pieces each; arrange them in a dry quart jar. Pour in the sugar, red chilli powder, and salt, and shake vigorously for 3 minutes to mix the ingredients.

Cover the bottle tightly with the lid. Place in the sun, outdoors preferably, or at a warm, sunny window. Stir every 4 to 5 days with a dry spoon.

The lime pickle will be ready in a couple of months. The longer it is kept in the sun, the more tender the lime will become.

Serve as a condiment. This pickle is especially good with yogurt-rice.

Green Chilli Pickle for the Daring

Munni Rodrigues

Editor's note: The hotness of the chilli will vary. You can choose very hot chillies, or, contrary to the title, relatively mild ones. This dish is best made in the summer when you get farm-fresh produce.

Makes enough to fill one 16-ounce bottle (keep a smaller bottle ready for the overflow)

½ pound dried tamarind
½ tablespoon fenugreek
  seeds
10 tablespoons black
  mustard seeds
7 tablespoons cumin
  seeds
3 cups mustard oil*
7 tablespoons ginger
  paste

7 tablespoons garlic
  paste
1 pound fresh green
  chillies, split length-
  wise
¼ cup salt
3 tablespoons sugar
2 cups white vinegar

*Mustard oil is often used for pickling and is also favored in the regional cuisines of northern and eastern India.

Soak the tamarind and extract the pulp to make ½ cup of thick liquid (To extract the tamarind pulp, follow instructions, p. 21.)

Dry-roast the fenugreek seeds, mustard seeds, and cumin seeds, and when they cool, grind finely. Set aside.

In a wok, heat the oil on medium high and fry the ginger and garlic paste for a few minutes. Add the ground spices (fenugreek, mustard seeds, cumin seeds), and ½ cup tamarind liquid Add the split green chillies, and the salt. Cook for about 20 minutes on medium. Add the sugar and vinegar and stir.

Cool the mixture and pour into a dry, sterile bottle with a wide mouth. Allow the pickle to mature for a week. The chillies should be tender.

Do not drain the oil since it acts as a preservative. When serving the pickle, however, take the chillies out with as little of the oil as possible.

Serve in a small bowl as a relish for any Indian meal.

ॐ
Desserts & Sweets

Desserts and sweets in India are very different from those in the West. Extremely sweet and mostly made with ghee (clarified butter), they are surely a sign of celebration. In fact, the Hindi/Urdu phrase "to sweeten the mouth" refers to a celebratory eating of sweets. Indian desserts have been compared to puddings. Often slow-cooked in milk till thick and creamy, they can be made with rice, semolina, legumes, wheat flour, gram flour, cracked wheat, noodles, paneer (homemade cheese similar to ricotta), and countless other foods. And then there are sweets—for the non-Indian palate, sometimes too perfumed and unsubtle. Cooked in syrup, or made as fudge or toffee or luscious balls, they may contain nuts, dried fruits, paneer, flour, or dal, to name just a few possibilities. Deep fried, simmered, slow-cooked; drenched in syrup; scented with rose water or other essences; flavored with cardamom or saffron; frequently colorful; often decorated with gossamer-thin, pure silver leaf and nuts; stacked in dazzling arrays at sweet shops—there appears to be no limit. Desserts are served most often with the rest of your meal, whereas sweets are served on high days and holidays; at celebrations and religious festivals and rituals; as tea-time snacks or when someone drops by. And although pastries, cakes, and pies are not part of traditional Indian cuisine, they are welcomed into the sweet tradition and enjoyed.

Elegant Rice & Milk Dessert
(Kheer)

Shuchi Agrawal

Contributor's note: Kheer is a traditional Indian dessert served on special occasions. Although made with rice and milk, it is *not* to be mistaken for plain old rice pudding!

Serves 4

¼ cup rice
½ cup cold water
5–6 almonds
1 tablespoon unsalted pistachios
1 tablespoon cashews
4 green cardamom pods
12–14 saffron threads

1 quart whole milk
1 teaspoon ghee (clarified butter)
2 teaspoons chiraunji seeds*
¼–½ cup sugar

*See glossary

Thoroughly rinse the rice and soak it in ½ cup water for 15 minutes. Drain the rice in a sieve for a couple of minutes.

Thinly slice the almonds, pistachios, and cashew nuts. Remove the skins from the cardamom pods and grind the seeds. Soak the saffron threads in 1 tablespoon of lukewarm milk. Set aside.

In a heavy saucepan, heat the ghee on medium; add the rice and fry for one minute. Stir in the milk and bring to a boil. Reduce the heat and cook on low for about 1 to 1½ hours. During this process, the milk should bubble very gently but not boil. Stir every 5 minutes until the rice grains are completely soft and the milk is very thick.

Add the sliced nuts, chiraunji, and sugar; stir, and cook for another minute. Turn off the heat. Add the saffron with its liquid and the ground cardamom, and stir gently.

Sprinkle a few chopped pistachios on top for garnish.

Chill before serving.

Sweet Saffron Rice

(Muza'fir/ Zarda)

Tasneem F. Husain

Editor's note: In Urdu, *Muza'fir* means tasty and *Zarda* means yellow. Either name is acceptable since the dessert is delicious, and saffron imparts a rich golden color to the rice. Yellow food coloring is often added or substituted for saffron although it lacks the delicate fragrance that saffron offers.

Serves 10–12

2 cups basmati rice
½ cup unsalted butter
¼ cup slivered almonds
3 tablespoons golden
 raisins
2 sticks of cinnamon
3 cloves

1½ cups water
Pinch of saffron
Yellow food coloring
 (optional)
¾ cup sugar
½ teaspoon green car-
 damom seeds, ground

Rinse and soak the rice for 30 minutes, then drain.

In a small frying pan, melt 1 tablespoon butter on low and fry the almonds and raisins. When the almonds turn golden and the raisins puff up, take out and set aside.

In a heavy saucepan, melt the remaining butter on medium. Add the cinnamon, cloves, and rice. Stir till the moisture evaporates from the rice.

Add 1½ cups water and saffron. If using food coloring, add to the water as well. Cover and simmer for 10 to 15 minutes till the water is absorbed and the rice is completely cooked through. Add the sugar and ground cardamom and gently mix well.

Transfer the rice to a serving dish and decorate with almonds and raisins.

Creamy Carrot Dessert
(Gajar ka Halva)

Yamuna Kachru

Adapted and reprinted with permission from *The International Linguistic Gourmet Cookbook,* 1976, compiled and produced by the Department of Linguistics, University of Illinois at Urbana-Champaign.

Serves 6

6 medium carrots, scraped & coarsely grated

4 cups milk

1 cup light cream

1 cup jaggery* (or substitute dark brown sugar combined with dark molasses)

½ cup sugar

1½–2 cups whole blanched almonds, pulverized in a blender or with a nut grinder

¼ cup ghee (clarified butter)

½ teaspoon green cardamom seeds, crushed

¼ cup unsalted pistachios, toasted

¼ cup unsalted, slivered, blanched almonds, toasted

*See glossary

In a deep, heavy 5–6 quart saucepan, combine the carrots, milk, and cream. Stirring constantly, bring to a boil over high heat. Reduce the heat to moderate, and stirring occasionally cook for 1 hour or until the mixture has reduced to about half its original volume and is thick enough to coat a spoon heavily.

Stir in the jaggery (or the brown sugar plus molasses) and the sugar, and continue cooking for 10 minutes. Reduce the heat to the lowest possible point, add the pulverized almonds and ghee, and stir for 10 minutes or more until the halva mixture is thick enough to draw away from the sides and bottom of the pan in a solid mass.

Remove the pan from the heat and stir in the cardamom. With a metal spatula, spread the halva on a large heat-proof platter, mound it slightly in the center, and decorate with pistachios and slivered almonds. Serve warm or at room temperature.

Comment: In India, *gajar ka halva* is also sometimes decorated with a special, edible, gossamer-thin silver leaf (see *vark* in glossary).

Semolina Halva
(Suji ka Halva)

Aradhna Chhajed

Serves 4–6

½ cup semolina (suji*)
½ cup whole wheat
   flour
8 tablespoons butter

1 cup hot water
1 cup sugar
Seeds of 3–4 green car-
   damom pods, ground

*See glossary

In a heavy pan, dry roast the semolina and flour on very low heat. Add the butter and sauté until the mixture pulls away from the edges of the pan (about 15 minutes).

Slowly add the hot water and stir in the sugar. Add the cardamom for garnish.

Serve warm or at room temperature.

Variations
- After the semolina is well fried, add a tablespoon each of raisins and slivered almonds and fry briefly before adding the hot water.
- Soak a few strands of saffron in a tablespoon of warm water, and add it to the pan when you add the hot water.

Apple Halva

Shuchi Agrawal

Serves 4–6

1½ pounds apples
2 green cardamom pods
2½ tablespoons ghee
  (clarified butter)
⅓ cup) assorted nuts
  (almonds, pistachios,

cashews &
  chiraunji*)
½ cup sugar or more as
  needed

*See glossary

Peel and grate the apples with a large-hole grater.

Peel the cardamoms and grind the seeds in the mortar. Set aside. Thinly slice the nuts.

In a wok, heat about 1 teaspoon of ghee and fry the sliced nuts for about a minute or until they become fragrant. Do not over-fry the nuts. Set aside.

In the same wok, heat about 2 tablespoons of ghee and fry the grated apples for 2 to 4 minutes on medium-high heat.

Reduce the heat, cover, and cook the grated apples until tender, stirring occasionally (about 15 minutes).

Add the sugar and nuts. Mix well and keep stirring until the liquid evaporates (about 2 to 4 minutes). Sprinkle with ground cardamom before serving.

Note: You can make squash (*lauki/doodhi*) halva the same way. Adjust the amount of sugar to taste.

Sweetened Gram Flour Balls
(Besan ke Laddu)

Urmila Chandra

Makes approximately 20–24 balls

3½ cups gram flour (besan)

1 cup melted ghee (clarified butter)

20 almonds, coarsely ground

20 cashew nuts, coarsely ground

2 cups sugar

½ teaspoon green cardamom seeds, ground

Sift the flour, and mix in the ghee by rubbing it well into the flour. In a karhai (or wok) or in a big frying pan roast the flour on medium heat till it becomes light brown and the ghee starts separating from it, and the mixture gives off a pleasant, roasted aroma.

Add the nuts and roast for another two minutes. Set aside and allow the mixture to cool down till it is lukewarm. (If the pan is too hot and the flour continues to cook and become darker, transfer the mixture to a plate to cool.)

Add sugar and ground cardamom and rub it into the besan with the palms of both hands till it is very well mixed. Take about 2 to 3 tablespoons at a time of the mixture and form into lime-sized balls (called *laddus*) by rolling the mixture in your palms.

Tip: Instead of gram flour, you can substitute whole-wheat flour. In that case, use 3 cups flour and 1¼ cups ghee. Follow the same method as above.

Gram Flour Fudge
(Besan ki Burfi)

Urmila Chandra

Makes approximately three-quarter pounds of fudge

3 cups gram flour
  (besan)
½ cup melted ghee
  (clarified butter) or oil
2 cups sugar

1 cup milk
Garnish: ½ tablespoon
  pistachios, chopped
½ teaspoon green car-
  damom seeds, ground

Mix the besan and ghee (or oil), rubbing them together to blend well.

Roast the mixture on medium heat, stirring continuously, till the besan turns light brown and gives off a pleasant roasted aroma. This should take about 5 to 8 minutes.

Add the sugar and keep stirring for one minute. Turn off the heat and add the milk. Stir thoroughly till the mixture resembles a thick soft dough.

Spread on a well-greased platter or in a 9-inch square dish; garnish with pistachio pieces and ground cardamom seeds.

When the burfi is set and cool, cut into 2-inch squares. The burfi can be kept unrefrigerated for 2 to 3 days. After that, it should be refrigerated.

Festive Apricot Dessert
(Hyderabadi Khubani ka Meetha)

Tasneem F. Husain

Contributor's note: This simple and delectable dessert is made with whole dried apricots and is traditionally served at Muslim weddings in Hyderabad in South India.

Serves 6

1 pound dried apricots, whole*

2 cups water

2 cups sugar (less if apricots are sweet)

½ teaspoon vanilla essence

1 teaspoon lemon juice

Garnish: Apricot seeds (kernels), chopped

*Available at Indian and international food and grocery stores.

Soak the whole apricots in water overnight.

Before cooking, cut the apricots open and remove the hard shell containing the seed from each apricot. Split open the shell and extract the seed (kernel). The apricot kernels resemble small almonds. Discard the shells and save the kernels.

In a saucepan add the water, sugar, and apricots. Cook on medium heat till the apricots are tender and the liquid starts to thicken and glaze (about 30 minutes). Remove from the heat and add the vanilla essence.

Chop the apricot kernels.

When the fruit has cooled, add 1 teaspoon of lemon juice and stir.

Garnish with the chopped apricot kernels.

This dish is often topped with custard. Vanilla ice cream or whipped topping are also alternatives.

Cottlestone Pie

Zarina Hock

Contributor's note: This is a kind of key-lime pie with a hint of Kewra, an essence typically used in special dishes in my home city of Lucknow. The dessert's unusual name comes from *Winnie the Pooh*, which I was reading to my five-year-old son during the time I invented this pie.

Serves: 4–6

1 prepared pie crust
1 egg white, lightly beaten
1–2 cups unflavored low-fat yogurt
4 ounces sweetened condensed milk or to taste
1 lime (1 teaspoon zest and 2 teaspoons juice)
½ teaspoon green cardamom seeds, freshly crushed
Kewra essence* (2–3 drops, max.)
Garnish: 1–2 teaspoons chopped pistachios (unsalted) or sliced almonds

*See glossary

Preheat oven to 250 degrees F.

Brush the pie crust with a thin coat of beaten egg white and bake according to package instructions. Cool on a wire rack.

Pie filling
In a bowl, whisk the yogurt till smooth. Add the condensed milk and mix well.

Use a grater to make the lime zest and add to the yogurt mixture. Add the lime juice a little at a time. Adjust the tartness according to your taste.

Mix in the cardamom and 2 to 3 drops of kewra essence. Be very careful not to overdo the kewra.

Pour the mixture into the baked pie crust and bake at 250 degrees F. for 30 minutes or until set.

When the mixture is firm, remove from the oven and sprinkle with chopped pistachios and/or almond slices.

Chill before serving.

Health tip: Use a reduced-fat pie crust and fat-free condensed milk.

Royal Fried Bread in Scented Cream
(Shahi Tukra)

Tasneem F. Husain

Editor's note: This is not just bread pudding, but a rich and creamy bread dessert served on very special occasions. Shahi Tukra is associated with the royal houses of Lucknow in the North and Hyderabad in the South. Traditionally, this dish is made with a form of condensed milk called *rabri*. Whole milk is slow-cooked until it turns very thick and creamy. Making rabri is a time-consuming process, so this recipe offers a shortcut.

Serves 8

10 slices thinly sliced white bread
6 ounces ghee (clarified butter)
½ cup almonds, thinly sliced
1 cup whole milk
1 pint heavy whipping cream or table cream
1¼ cup sugar (or to taste)
A pinch of saffron ground
½ teaspoon cardamom powder
2 tablespoons pistachios, sliced
½ cup yellow raisins

Preheat oven to 350 degrees F.

Carefully trim the crust off each slice of bread and cut diagonally to make triangles. Set aside.

In a frying pan, heat a little ghee and fry the almonds till light brown. Set aside.

In the same pan, add the remaining ghee a little at a time and shallow-fry the bread in batches. Arrange the slices in a glass baking dish.

Mix together the milk, whipping cream, sugar, saffron, and cardamom powder and bring to a boil. Pour the mixture over the bread evenly. Add more milk if the bread is not fully soaked.

Sprinkle the almonds, pistachios, and raisins over the milk-drenched bread and bake in a preheated oven for 20 minutes.

Serve chilled.

Reminder: This dessert is very rich. It might be worth cutting back on some other foods when you plan to indulge in Shahi Tukra!

Fried Milk Balls in Rose-Scented Syrup

(Gulab Jamun)

Rajeshwari Pandharipande

Serves 6–8

For the syrup
3 cups sugar
5 cups water
1 teaspoon green cardamom seeds, ground
1 teaspoon rose water

For the jamuns

2 cups powdered milk
  (nonfat Carnation*)
1 cup Bisquick
4 tablespoons melted
  butter

½ cup milk
1–2 cups oil or vegetable
  shortening for deep-
  frying

*This brand of powdered milk works best for this recipe.

The syrup: Mix the sugar with the water and bring to a boil. Lower the heat and add the ground cardamom and rose water. Keep the syrup warm.

The jamuns: Knead together the powdered milk, Bisquick, melted butter, and milk, and make the mix into balls the size of tiny apricots.

In a karhai (or wok), heat the oil on medium. Deep-fry the balls on low heat till they are a rich brown. Drain on paper towels. Do not let the balls cool down!

Gently slide the balls into the syrup and let them sit for 3 to 4 hours. Serve warm or cold.

Almond Fudge (1)
(Badaam ki Burfi)

Nandini Pai

Makes 24–30 squares

1 cup almonds (soaked and peeled)
1 cup skim milk (2% milk for richer recipe)
⅓ cup water
1½ cups sugar
4 tablespoons unsalted butter
½ to 1 teaspoon green cardamom seeds, ground
1–2 pinches powdered saffron
1 teaspoon of ghee (clarified butter) or oil

In a blender or food processor, grind the almonds with the milk to make a paste. Pour into a half-gallon, microwave-safe bowl.

Use the ⅓ cup water to rinse out the blender cup; and add it to the almond paste.

Add the sugar and butter to the almond paste.

Put the bowl in the microwave at high power (level 10) for 5 to 10 minutes, depending on your microwave. (Use the longer time for a smaller microwave.) Make sure that the paste does not overflow. If the paste rises up, stir to keep it from boiling over.

Heat the paste for 10 minutes at reduced power (level 8) or 5 minutes at full power (level 10), while watching for overflow. Add the cardamom and saffron. Stir as often as needed.

Continue cooking in 5-minute spurts at least twice more, stirring occasionally. The whole cooking process should take 28 to 30 minutes, depending on the strength of your microwave oven. When cooked, the almond paste should look golden, and the consistency should be somewhat thick and sticky.

While the paste is cooking, grease an 8-inch square glassware cake dish with ghee or oil. Pour the paste into the glass dish and spread it evenly with a greased spatula or the back of a spoon.

Cool and cut into squares.

Almond Fudge (2)
(Badaam ki Burfi)

Indra Aggarwal

Editor's note: You can either buy paneer (available at Indian grocery stores) or make it yourself. Of course, homemade is much better, and the contributor makes her own. To make paneer, see p 20.

Serves 4

10 ounces paneer*
1 stick unsalted butter
1 cup sweetened con-
   densed milk
1 cup sugar

1 cup ground almonds
2 teaspoons chopped
   pistachios
½ teaspoon green car-
   damom seeds, ground

*You will have to make this ahead of time. See headnote.

Mash the paneer until smooth.

Lightly grease a cookie sheet with a little butter.

In a saucepan on low heat, melt the remaining butter; add the paneer, condensed milk, sugar, and almonds. Stir and cook for 5 to 10 minutes on low heat.

Spread the mixture on the buttered cookie sheet. Sprinkle with chopped pistachios and ground cardamom. Let the mixture set at room temperature for several hours.

Cut into diamonds or squares before serving.

Sweet Vermicelli Supreme
(Sevaiyan ka Muza'fir)

Tasneem F. Husain

Editor's note: Sevaiyan is served at the celebration marking the end of Ramadan; but it is enjoyed by all groups in India as well. I recall that when growing up in Lucknow, our communities—Christian, Hindu, and Muslim—would exchange special sweets on our individual holidays. My mother would send over her Christmas cake to non-Christian friends, and we would receive special *mithai* (sweets) at Diwali, the Hindu Festival of Lights, and sevaiyan on Eid ul Fitr. A sweet arrangement indeed.

Serves 6

2 sticks unsalted butter
2½ cups vermicelli broken up (*sevaiyan*)
1 cup almonds (slivered)
4 whole green cardamom pods
2 sticks cinnamon
4 cloves
1 cup hot water
1 cup Carnation milk powder (or khoa, a dried milk product*)
1½ cups milk

2½ cups sugar
Pinch of saffron, ground and soaked in 1 teaspoon water
½ teaspoon cardamom powder
Garnish: ½ cup yellow raisins
¼ cup pitted dates, chopped (optional)

*See glossary

In a 5-quart pot, on medium heat, melt the butter Add the vermicelli and almonds and fry till lightly browned.

Add cardamom, cinnamon, and cloves, followed by the hot water.

Mix the milk powder or khoa with the milk and pour the mixture into the pan, stirring lightly. As the vermicelli absorbs the milk, add the sugar. Cook on low heat till the sugar dissolves, constantly stirring. Add saffron and cardamom powder. Stir gently. Cover and simmer for 10 to 12 minutes. Garnish with raisins and, if using, dates.

Sweetened Paneer Balls in Light Syrup
(Rasgulla)

Indra Aggarwal

Editor's note: You can either buy paneer (available at Indian grocery stores) or make it yourself. Of course, homemade is much better, and the contributor makes her own. To make paneer, see p. 20. This dish is best made in a pressure cooker.

Makes 18 balls

10 ounces paneer*   4 cups water
2 cups sugar   ***See headnote**

Mash the paneer until smooth and form into balls, 1½ inches in diameter (about 18 balls).

Mix the sugar and water and boil in a pressure cooker without the weight on it. When the syrup starts boiling, slide the balls in, cover and apply the weight to the cooker. As soon as the pressure cooker starts to whistle, reduce the heat to medium and cook for 10 minutes.

Take the cooker from the stove and hold under cold running water. After all the steam escapes, remove the cover. Let the contents cool at room temperature. Then refrigerate.

Serve chilled.

Indian Ice Cream
(Quick Kulfi)

Zohreh Sullivan

Editor's note: This is a quick and easy way to make kulfi, a frozen dessert similar to ice cream, which is popular in India and Pakistan. Traditionally, kulfi is not made with bread. This version is much easier to make, and the end result is still delicious.

Serves 4–6

1 12-ounce can condensed milk
1 12-ounce can evaporated milk
1½ cups regular milk
2 slices of white bread, with crusts removed
½ teaspoon green cardamom seeds, ground
½ teaspoon powdered saffron
2 teaspoons slivered almonds and pistachios
⅓ cup cream

In a saucepan, mix the condensed, evaporated, and regular milk and add the bread slices. Mash the bread well into the milk. Add the cardamom, saffron, and the nuts. Boil for 5 minutes and then cool.

Add the cream and freeze in cone-shaped containers.

Sprinkle with cardamom and pistachios before serving.

Variation: Add mango purée to the mix before freezing. (Canned mango purée is available at Indian and international food and grocery stores.)

Tofu Kaju (Cashew) Delight

Kavitha Reddy

Adapted and reprinted with permission from *The Indian Soy Cookbook* by Kavitha Reddy, American Soybean Association, 2002. The contributor has provided nutritional information at the end of the recipe.

Serves 6

½ pound tofu
¼ pound cashew nuts, pulverized
1½ cups condensed milk
½ teaspoon ground green cardamom seeds

1 tablespoon chopped pistachios
Saffron, a few strands
Garnish: Silver leaf (*vark**) if available

*See glossary

Mash the tofu with a fork. Add the pulverized cashew nuts and mix well.

Heat a heavy-bottomed pan on medium-low, add the condensed milk and the tofu-cashew mixture. Cook, stirring continuously, till the mixture starts to pull away from the sides of the pan and collects in the center.

Stir in the cardamom, remove, and pour into a greased serving dish. Garnish with chopped pistachios, saffron strands, and, if available, silver leaf. Allow the mixture to cool, and cut into small squares.

Nutritional value per serving: Calories 355 kcal; protein 11.2 gm; carbohydrate 43.7 gm; fat 16.5 gm.

Fragrant Ricotta in Sweet Cream
(Ras Malaai)

Tasneem F. Husain

Editor's note: Ras Malaai is a celestial dessert—richly creamy and yet delicate in flavor. This recipe offers a quick way to get the same results. It is worth skimping on some other foods if you plan to eat ras malaai at the end of your meal.

Serves 4–6

1 pound ricotta cheese
1 cup sugar
1 cup half and half
  cream & milk
¼ cup almonds, finely
  sliced

1 pinch ground green
  cardamom
1 tablespoon pistachios,
  finely sliced
1 pinch saffron

Preheat oven to 325 degrees F.

Mix the ricotta cheese well with ⅛ cup of sugar and spread in a pan. Press down firmly with a spatula. Bake for about 20 to 25 minutes or until set but NOT brown.

Remove from the oven and cool. Cut the baked ricotta into 2-inch pieces and place in a deep serving dish or bowl.

In a saucepan, mix the half and half, the remaining sugar, the almonds, and ground cardamom, and cook on low heat. Bring to a gentle boil and cook for 6 to 8 minutes.

Pour the milk over the ricotta pieces in the serving dish. Sprinkle with pistachios and saffron.

Chill for at least 3 hours or overnight before serving.

Tropical Delight

Tasneem F. Husain

Editor's note: This is a light and quick summer dessert that looks colorful and is the perfect end to a spicy meal on a warm summer evening.

Serves 8

1 20-ounce can mango pulp*

1 16-ounce container whipped topping

1 cup milk

3 cups vanilla ice cream

2 cans tropical fruit or fresh fruits (fresh mangoes if available)

*Available at Indian and international food and grocery stores.

Mix together the mango pulp, whipped topping, milk, and ice cream.

Top with sliced fruit and serve.

ℭℛ
Beverages

Hot and cold drinks are popular in India—some sweet, some savory, some spicy. Beverages and juices are not served with traditional meals and neither are alcoholic drinks. Further, tea and coffee are not normally offered at the end of a meal. But both are enjoyed in India. While coffee is the favored drink of South India, tea is more popular in the North, where hot tea is enjoyed regardless of hot or cold weather. Nothing revives one more at breakfast, morning break, or tea-time than a strong cup of black tea served with milk and sugar. Other teas offer comfort as well. Kashmiri tea (kehwa) is renowned as an elegant brew consisting of green tea, almonds, saffron, and other delicate spices. Masala chai, drunk especially in the winter months, is tea spiked with spices and herbs. Aromatic coffee comes from the coffee plantations of the South. The flavor, as contributor Vijaya Jain reminded me, is enhanced because the ground coffee is first filtered before being added to heated milk. Finally, there is "cold coffee" (often made with instant coffee), which is immensely popular with the younger generation, both in the South and the North. (Iced tea, however, is alien to India.)

Mango-Yogurt Drink
(Mango Lassi)

Manisha Bhagwat

Serves 4–6

4 cups yogurt
1 cup mango pulp, fresh
   or canned
2–3 cups water

2–4 tablespoons sugar
Pinch of green carda-
   mom seeds, ground
Garnish: Saffron strands

In a blender or with a hand blender beat the yogurt, mango pulp, and water till smooth.

Taste the mixture and add sugar as needed and then blend again.

Stir the ground cardamom into the lassi. Refrigerate.

Serve cold in tall glasses with a couple of saffron strands on the top for garnish.

Mango-Soy Milkshake

Kavitha Reddy

Adapted and reprinted with permission from *The Indian Soy Cookbook* by Kavitha Reddy, American Soybean Association, 2002. The contributor has provided nutritional information at the end of the recipe.

Serves 5

½ pound fresh ripe
  mangoes

Sugar to taste
4 cups soymilk

Wash, peel, and chop the mangoes. Place chopped mangoes, sugar, and 1 cup of soymilk in a blender jar. Blend to a smooth paste.

Add the mango paste to the remaining soymilk and strain through a muslin cloth. Discard the residue. Refrigerate the milkshake and garnish with mango slices just before serving.

Nutritional value per serving: Calories 152 kcal; protein 4.3 gm; carbohydrate 33.4 gm; fat 1.4 gm.

Soy-Coconut Drink

Kavitha Reddy

Adapted and reprinted with permission from *The Indian Soy Cookbook* by Kavitha Reddy, American Soybean Association, 2002. The contributor has provided nutritional information at the end of the recipe.

Serves 2

1 cup soymilk
½ cup coconut milk
½ cup vanilla ice cream

Sugar to taste (for those on sugar-free diets, use sweetener as needed)

Place all the ingredients in a blender; blend to combine. Serve with crushed ice.

Nutritional value per serving: Calories 293 kcal; protein 6.6 gm; carbohydrate 32 gm; fat 16.8 gm.

Savory Cumin Punch
(Jal Jeera or Jeera Paani)

Manisha Bhagwat

Contributor's note: Literally translated, the name means *cumin water.* This drink can be served as a savory punch or an appetizer. It is a refreshing summer drink.

Serves 4–6

2 tablespoons tamarind pulp*
8 cups water
1 tablespoon fresh mint
1 tablespoon fresh ginger
¼ cup fresh lemon juice
1 tablespoon dry-roasted ground cumin (jeera)*

1 teaspoon red chilli powder
½ teaspoon garam masala
2 teaspoons black salt ‡
2–3 tablespoons sugar
3–4 lemon slices
3–4 sprigs of mint

* To prepare these ingredients, see pages 20–22.
‡ **See glosssary**

Mix the tamarind pulp and water. Grind the mint and ginger with the lemon juice, and add the ground dry-roasted cumin, red chilli powder, garam masala, and black salt.

Add the mint-ginger paste to the tamarind water and whisk well. Add the sugar and taste for tartness. This spicy drink is supposed to be sweet and sour. Pour the mixture through a fine-mesh strainer.

Refrigerate and serve cold with lemon slices and sprigs of mint.

Ginger Hot Drink

Zarina Hock

Contributor's note: A popular home remedy for colds and sore throat, this drink originates in Ayurvedic medicine (see p.16). It is not conventional ginger tea since it is usually made with whole crushed dried ginger and without regular tea leaves. A soothing hot drink in winter, the ingredients added to the ginger may vary.

Serves 6

1-inch piece fresh ginger or, preferably, dried whole ginger (*sonth*) if available (this is stronger)

A few peppercorns
8–9 cups cold water
Fresh lemon juice
Honey to taste

If using fresh ginger, peel and pound with a mortar and pestle. If using sonth, crush the whole pieces before cooking. Put the peppercorns and crushed ginger in a medium saucepan with 8–9 cups of water. Bring to a boil, cover and simmer for 10 to 15 minutes or longer if you wish.

Strain and serve hot with a generous squeeze of lemon juice and a dollop of honey.

Kashmiri Green Tea
(Kehwa)

Nancy Zutshi

Contributor's note: For Kashmiri green tea, the dried whole leaves are, ideally, hand crushed in bulk. The tea leaves may be available at international food and grocery stores or can be ordered online.

Makes 4 cups

Note: A very small quantity of tea leaves is required, and using a larger amount will make for a bitter brew.

4–6 cups cold water
3–4 green cardamom
  pods
1 stick cinnamon
2–3 threads of saffron

¼ teaspoon Kashmiri
  green tea leaves,
  crushed
Slivered almonds
Sugar to taste

In a saucepan, boil 4 to 6 cups of water with the cardamom, cinnamon, and saffron. Let the water boil for a good 2 to 3 minutes. Add the tea leaves, bring to a boil and remove immediately from the heat. Cover and let the tea steep for 5 minutes in the saucepan.

Pour into cups and garnish with slivered almonds. Serve with sugar to taste.

Masala Chai

Shuchi Agrawal

Contributor's note: Chai (Indian tea) is chai! It cannot be bound by season. A year-round favorite, it is made in many households in North India. Chai is one of the most well known of Indian drinks; almost all my western friends not only know this kind of tea but also call it *chai.*

Serves 4

2–4 cloves
4 black peppercorns
2–3 green cardamom
　pods
3 cups water
1½ teaspoons grated
　fresh ginger

4 teaspoons sugar (or to
　taste)
3 teaspoons black tea or
　4 tea bags
1½ cups milk

Grind the cloves and black pepper in a mortar and set aside. Grind the green cardamom pods with their skins in the mortar and set aside.

Boil the water with the grated ginger, sugar, ground cloves and black pepper. After approximately two minutes of boiling, add black tea and boil for 30 seconds.

Add milk and ground cardamom and bring to a boil again.

Strain and serve.

A Classic Cuppa
(A Real Cup of Tea)

Zarina Hock

Contributor's note: One of the most frustrating experiences for me when I came to the United States was ordering a cup of tea at a restaurant. Hot tea at that time (some decades ago) was almost unknown. And iced tea was not something I enjoyed. We've come a long way since then, and hot tea (of sorts) is available, but without milk unless requested. Here is how I make tea in my home. Nowadays, both in India and elsewhere, teabags are replacing loose-leaf tea. You can follow the same process, using tea bags if you wish.

Makes 5 cups

You will need: A 6-cup teapot, a tea cozy,* and a tea strainer.

*A padded, quilted, or thick cloth covering for a teapot, which looks rather like a quaint hat.

6 cups of cold, fresh water (not preheated water of any temperature)

5 teaspoons tea leaves (Darjeeling or Assam or other black tea of your choice)
Hot milk for the tea
Sugar optional

In a tea kettle, bring the water to a rolling boil. Pour a little water into the teapot to warm it. Drain, then put the tea leaves in the teapot and fill with five cups of water. Put the lid on, and cover the pot with a tea cozy. Steep 5 to 7 minutes, depending on how strong you like your tea. (Darjeeling is a delicate tea that stays fairly light unless soaked very long. Assam tea is much stronger and you may want it lighter.)

Heat the milk and pour into a small milk pitcher. Pour a little milk into the teacup. When the tea is ready, stir and pour it through the strainer into the teacup. (Some people prefer to add the milk after the tea is poured.) Add sugar if you prefer sweetened tea.

Options

(1) Add green cardamom to the teapot when you put in the leaves. The cardamom should be slightly crushed so the seeds are exposed. Let the cardamom steep with the leaves. You can also add fresh mint leaves or lemongrass or peeled fresh ginger, finely chopped.

(2) Yet another way of brewing tea is to bring the water to a boil in a saucepan and to add the tea, milk, sugar (if you are using it) and cardamom—all together—to the boiling water. Bring to a second boil and remove from the heat and serve.

Kulhar ki Chai
(Tea in a Clay Cup or The Best Tea in the World)

For some of us who grew up in India, the most delectable of teas was the tea sold at railway stations. As our train would shudder to a stop at a platform, vendors would materialize at the train window offering steaming hot, sweet tea brewed with rich milk served in clay cups. The distinctive flavor of warm, moist clay was both comforting and restorative. The cups were immediately biodegradable and for us as children it was a delight to fling the cups out of the windows into the fields that whizzed by when our train took off. Sadly, with modernization in present-day India, tea on stations is now served in thermoses.

Glossary

(Internet sources consulted for glossary definitions have been checked for accuracy.)

Ajwain. Usually goes by this (Indian) name. The English names, Bishop's Weed or Carom, are rarely used. Often an ingredient in breads and salty snacks, ajwain is also considered a digestive in India.

Amchur. Raw, dried mango in powdered form. Used as a souring agent in Indian cooking.

Asafoetida or **Asafetida.** See **Hing** or **Heeng.**

Basmati Rice. Fragrant, long-grained rice, originally cultivated in North India at the foot of the Himalaya mountains. It is difficult to go wrong with rice if you use basmati. Texas now produces a cross-bred rice called Texmati, also long-grained and aromatic, but not quite basmati!

Besan. Chickpea flour, also known as **gram** flour.

Bharta. Typically, this dish consists of a single mashed vegetable (not a blend) prepared with spices. Roasted eggplant is a very popular choice for a bharta. Potatoes or tomatoes are also used.

Black Cumin (Kala Jeera, also **Shah Zeera).** Different from regular **Cumin.** A tiny, flavorful seed similar in taste and looks to caraway. Often confused with nigella (black onion seed) from which it differs completely in taste.

Black Onion Seeds (Kalaunji). Also called nigella. Resembles black cumin but is completely different in taste. Used in **Panch Phoran** (five-spice) recipes. Also a pickling spice.

Black Salt. An unrefined salt used in Indian cooking, considered good for digestion. Black salt has a strong sulphuric flavor. Often used in condiments and snacks. Black salt comes as a rock salt or powdered. As a powder, it can lose its flavor if not kept tightly bottled.

Cardamom. There are two kinds—green and black cardamom. **Green cardamom**, with a light green pod, is widely used in both sweet and savory dishes. The pod is used whole in many dishes, and for other dishes the seeds are separated and ground. The seeds are also eaten along with fennel and clove as a mouth freshener. **Black cardamom**, resembling a rather large beetle, is mostly used in curries, pullaos, and some garam masalas but not in sweets. Cardamom, like many Indian spices, is considered to have medicinal properties.

Chaat, Chaat Masala. Chaat refers to a range of salty and spicy snack foods. The mixture of spices often used with salty snack foods is thus chaat masala. Usually sprinkled dry over the snack. You can find many chaat masala recipes on the web.

Chai, also **Cha** in North India. Chai means "tea." So the usage "chai tea" literally means "tea tea." In India, you just use one or the other word for plain tea, and "masala chai" for spiced tea.

Chana Dal. A variety of chickpeas. Also called **gram** (sometimes Bengal gram) in English. Gram flour is commonly used in India. See **Dals.**

Chickpeas. Also called **chana dal** or **gram.** Chickpeas come in large and small varieties. Large chickpeas are also called garbanzos, and the smaller size called **chana.**

Chilli. This does not refer to the meat-and-beans dish "chili" but to the hot peppers used in Indian and Mexican cooking. **Chilli Peppers** (also known as **Chili Pepper**, **Chillie**, and **Chile**) come in different varieties, shapes, colors, sizes, and intensities of hotness. Some can be eaten as vegetables (e.g., bell or sweet pepper); others are essential as spices. Red chilli peppers can be used fresh or dried (whole, crushed, or powdered), depending on the recipe. International and Indian groceries carry generic red chilli powder, as well as variety-specific ones, e.g., cayenne pepper or Kashmiri chilli powder (see **Kashmiri Mirch**).

Chiraunji. A small seed somewhat similar in taste to the almond. Popular in Indian sweets and desserts but also used in other dishes.

Cilantro. Called **Green Coriander** in India. Same as Chinese Parsely. An ingredient in its own right, adding much flavor to Indian dishes such as "masala" omelettes and some curries. Extremely popular as a garnish, especially for Indian foods in the West. Has a strong flavor that can be overwhelming in large quantities.

Coconut. Though high in saturated fat, coconut is irresistible when it is used in savory curries or sweets. Coconut flakes or pieces are available in Indian and international food and grocery stores. Canned coconut milk is also easily available. The coconut palm tree is the source of a vast range of products, not just those that are edible.

Coriander. Refers to the seeds of the coriander plant, which are popular in Indian cooking, both ground and whole. See also **Green Coriander,** which refers to the leaves of the coriander plant. The leaves have a very different flavor from the seeds and are popular as a garnish.

Cumin (Indian name **Jeera** or **Zeera**). An essential ingredient in Indian cuisine. Both variants of the Indian names are acceptable in India and have been used according to the contributor's preference in this publication. Originally, pronounced *jeera,* the word has been Persianized in some areas to *zeera.* Not the same as **Black Cumin** (see entry).

When *dry-roasted and ground,* cumin produces a smoky flavor that is different from that of regular ground cumin. Dry-roasted ground cumin is frequently sprinkled on foods or mixed in savory dishes. Use sparingly because it can overwhelm other flavors. To prepare, see p. 20.

Curry. In the United States, curry often is erroneously assumed to be a spice. This is understandable: Cinnamon powder, after all, is ground cinnamon; and cardamom powder is ground cardamom. So naturally, people assume that curry powder is derived from a spice called curry. But it isn't. Curry is, in fact, a method of cooking, similar in its end result to a stew. Curry powder is a combination of ground spices that one uses to flavor a curry. According to K. T. Achaya, (*Indian Food: A Historical Companion*), the word is derived from the South Indian (Tamil) word *kari* which originally referred to a pepper-spiced dish. Others ascribe it to a Tamil word meaning sauce. Later, it was Anglicized by the British and was applied to almost any spiced dish with a sauce or gravy.

Spice combinations vary with each curry and each cook. The spices in curries could include turmeric, ground cumin and coriander seeds, red chilli powder, mustard seeds, and many others, which are ground and combined. It is popularly believed that the British when relinquishing India (understandably) needed to take back some spices to improve their rather bland cuisine. So bottled curry powder is what they claimed as their last bounty. Packaged curry powder is typically not used in Indian households; instead, individual ground spices are combined ad hoc to suit the dish being prepared.

Curry leaves. Not the same as the dish called curry or curry powder. These are aromatic leaves resembling small bay leaves but with a different and strong flavor. Used both in meat and vegetarian cooking in India. Also called *sweet neem* because of the resemblance to neem leaves. Can be used dry or fresh. The dried leaves can be ground with whole spices. Often used when the fresh leaves are not available, though not as aromatic. The fresh leaves add brightness and a distinctive flavor to foods.

Dals. Generic term for legumes including peas, split beans, and pulses. There are numerous types of dals (hulled and split) and beans (whole), each with its own distinctive character and flavor. Space does not allow a more detailed description here. Among the most commonly used are **chana, lobhia, masoor, moong, rajma, toor,** and **urad.** Dals are a rich source of protein and thus constitute an essential part of a vegetarian diet in South Asia. They are also high in fiber. They are often seasoned with asafoetida and/or ginger and other natural aids to enhance digestibility. The terms *dal-bhaat* (dal and rice) or *dal-roti* (dal and bread) are used to signify your basic meal (like "daily bread" in English). See individual dal entries.

Drumstick. Not a musical instrument but a popular vegetable in India. "Drumsticks" are pods from a tropical tree native to India. All parts of the tree (pods, leaves, seeds) are said to be exceptionally nutritious. They can be cooked like green beans but also curried.

Dry. The term *dry* is commonly used in Indian cooking (and languages) to describe a dish that does not have a sauce or gravy. It does not mean "dried up." "*Wet*" indicates foods that have a sauce or gravy.

Fenugreek. See **Methi.**

Garam Masala. In Hindi, *garam* means warm, and *masala* means spice. Various interpretations are given for the choice of the term *garam*, so rather than speculate let's focus on the seasoning itself. Garam masala is a combination of selected whole spices, some of which are dry roasted, and all of which are ground together. Every cook has a favorite combination. Prepackaged garam masalas are widely available, and the combinations are legion. Garam masala is fragrant rather than pungent, and a very small quantity is typically added to the dish at the very end of the cooking stage (though sometimes added earlier or used in some marinades). See pages 13 and 20.

Ghee. Clarified butter made from milk fats. As recorded in scholarly and sacred Hindu texts that go back to 1500 BCE, ghee has been used in traditional cooking and religious rituals in India for millennia. Remarkable in flavor, it is also high in saturated fat. You may substitute vegetable oil for ghee though you will never get the same aroma and flavor!

Ginger, Fresh and **Ginger Powder.** Extremely popular in Indian and East Asian cooking, fresh ginger is now readily available in most grocery stores. Ginger powder is made from dried ginger (*sonth*) and has a somewhat different flavor from fresh ginger. Some regional cuisines, such as Kashmiri cooking, favor ginger powder. Ginger is said to have many medicinal properties and is used in hot drinks as a cold remedy and also considered a digestive aid.

Gojju. A savory vegetable dish from South India, with a thick gravy made with vegetables and a blend of tamarind, jaggery, and a few other spices. Cooked without lentils. Seasonal vegetables constitute the basis of the gravy, and any vegetable that is used lends its unique taste to the dish. For recipes, see pages 179 and 180.

Gram. Cover term for various legumes, such as chick-peas, green gram, black gram or urad bean, red gram, Bengal gram or chickpea. Each has its distinctive flavor and characteristics, and is a source of vegetarian protein.

Gur. See **Jaggery.**

Halva or **Halwa.** There are several types of sweets called halva, most of which come from the Middle East or West Asia. South Asian halvas are different. They are more like puddings (though denser), and can be made from vege-tables, different kinds of flour, fruit, nuts, and dals.

Hing or **Heeng (Asafoetida).** A hard, resinous substance with a startlingly distinct odor that many find unpleas-ant. Yet when cooked in tiny quantities, the aroma changes and is very appealing! The gum-like substance must be powdered before use. Packaged powdered hing is also available, but you can never be sure of its purity since it is commonly adulterated with other edible sub-stances. It also loses some of its odor when powdered. Hing is used very sparingly—just a pinch, which is fried rapidly and mixed with other spices. It is considered a digestive aid and said to have other medicinal properties as well. Often used in bean and lentil dishes. You either love it or hate it. (See the web for some fascinating details about hing.)

Jaggery. Also called **Gur.** A raw sugar usually derived from sugar cane or certain palm trees. It comes in a block, so you will need to grate or scrape it. Ranges in color from light to dark brown.

Jeera or **Zeera.** See **Cumin.**

Kabab. Same as kabobs. Skewered or cubed meats, often grilled. Also refers to Indian-style meat patties.

Karhai (also **Kadhai**). Similar to a wok, though more rounded and with less steep sides and usually heavier. Used for deep frying and stir frying.

Kashmiri Mirch. A chilli powder made from dried red chillies grown in the mountain regions of North India, including Kashmir. It imparts a bright red color to the food and is usually mild to moderately hot. It is often used in tandoori foods and in curries.

Kasoori Methi. See Methi.

Kewra. This essence is extracted from the flower of the Screw Pine tree, which is not a pine but a tropical tree, *pandanus utilis.* It is used to flavor meats, drinks, desserts, and pullaos, especially in Lucknow cuisine. It is highly scented, so you should use only a few drops, or the scent will be overpowering and the taste turn somewhat bitter.

Khoa or **Khoya.** A concentrated milk product that is made by cooking milk until it thickens and becomes fudge-like. Often used in sweet dishes.

Masala means spice. Masala can refer to a combination of spices mixed together for a specific dish or simply to the generic word *spice.* (The film *Mississippi Masala* was a romantic comedy about an Indian woman and an African American man in a romance that was in fact very spicy.)

Masoor Dal. Red lentils, considered an everyday dal. Cooks quickly, is more digestible than many dals, and is good in soups. See **Dals.**

Methi is fenugreek in English. The fresh greens, dried leaves **(kasoori methi)**, and seeds are said to have many health benefits. Methi has a strong and unusual flavor, which is widely liked in India. The distinctive flavor is sometimes considered too strong for those new to it. If you dry-roast the seeds, the flavor is enhanced and the bitterness reduced. The dry leaves are often reconstituted or added dry to vegetarian and meat dishes. Fresh methi greens are prepared like spinach. Methi is rich in lysine, an essential amino acid. From ancient times, fenugreek has been touted in various cultures as a remedy for ailments including arthritis, digestive ailments, and diabetes. In India, methi seeds are considered particularly effective in reducing high blood-glucose levels. The seeds are soaked in water overnight, and the methi-flavored water (drained of seeds) is drunk the following morning, on an empty stomach.

Moong or **Mung Beans/Dal.** A small yellow lentil with an olive green skin. You can buy whole moong beans with the skin on, or washed moong (referred to as a *dal*), which is split and skinless. Moong dal cooks quickly and is easier to digest than some other beans and dals. Moong beans sprout easily and are frequently used in light, salad-type dishes.

Mustard Seeds, Black. Widely used whole to season vegetables, particularly in the southern and the eastern regions. Also used in Indian pickles. When added to hot oil, they sputter and pop and release their flavor. Over-frying will destroy this flavor if other foods are not added immediately.

Panch Phoran Masala. A blend of five aromatic seeds—cumin, black mustard, fenugreek, fennel, and black onion (nigella) seeds. Commonly used in Bengal and other eastern regions of India, it is now popular elsewhere as well. The ratios will vary, depending on the dish and according to each cook's preference. The spices are added to hot oil to flavor both the oil and whatever vegetables you may add in a process called tarka. See **Tarka;** also p. 23.

Paneer or **Panir.** Homemade unripened cheese, sometimes confusingly referred to in restaurants as "cottage cheese." Paneer is a milk-based source of protein and popular in vegetarian cuisines. (For recipe, see p. 20). Paneer is used in both sweet and savory dishes.

Papadums or **Papads.** There are several regional variations of the name for this crisp, spicy/salty cracker-like flatbread made from lentil, bean, or rice flour and spices. Often served in Indian restaurants in the West as an appetizer, it can be deep fried or roasted. In India, papadums are served along with the meal.

Pressure Cooker. Cooking utensil widely used by Indians both in India and abroad. However, you can always use a regular pot, keeping in mind that the cooking time will be longer and the dish will need more cooking liquid than required in a pressure cooker.

Pullao, Pulao, Pulau, Pilaf. Always considered festive, this rice dish could involve frying or baking the rice, and any or all of the following: adding meat and/or vegetables; cooking in yogurt or in a specially prepared broth (*yakhni*); flavoring the rice with cumin, black cardamom, saffron, and other whole spices; garnishing the rice with nuts and raisins. Served with at least one dish containing liquid/sauce/gravy or with raita or plain yogurt.

Raita. A yogurt dish served as an accompaniment to most Indian meals. The name resists translation. In texture and style, raita is rather like a salad and dip combined. It contains vegetables and sometimes little dumplings. For more, see *Salads & Raitas,* p. 233.

Rajma. Red kidney beans. Canned kidney beans work well in curries. See **Dals.**

Rasam Powder. Ingredients for a South Indian soup-like dish, the powder can also season other dishes. See pages 179 and 226.

Sambar Powder. A spice mix for a South Indian soup/ stew-like dish called sambar (p. 125). The mix combines ground roasted whole spices (such as cumin, coriander, whole cinnamon, cloves fenugreek, poppy seeds), whole red chillies, gram, and turmeric. Sambar mixes are often made at home, but packaged ones are also available at Indian or international food stores.

Silver Leaf (Edible). See **Vark.**

Star Anise. Popular in East Asian cooking, this spice is more commonly used in North India than in the South, usually in meat or rice dishes. Star shaped with what looks like petals, it is hard and dark brown; somewhat similar in taste to anise. Use sparingly.

Suji or **Sooji.** Same as semolina. Though known in the United States as Cream of Wheat, it is used in Indian cooking to make delicious desserts and savory dishes, including crèpes.

Tamarind. Tart fruit (in a pod) of the tamarind tree. Tamarind is widely used as a souring agent and preservative both in North and South India for all kinds of foods from chutneys to main dishes and even in sweets. For process to extract tamarind juice, see p. 21.

Tandoori Masala. Spices for a special North and Northwest Indian cuisine that requires cooking the food in a clay oven called a tandoor. Meats, breads, and vegetables are spiced with tandoori masala and baked at high temperatures. Tandoori foods are similar to grilled foods and do not have a gravy. They are less greasy than fried foods. Aromatic and flavorful, tandoori food has become extremely popular in the West, and most South Asian restaurants are equipped with tandoors. Although you cannot quite replicate the flavor in a regular oven, you can buy tandoori spices to marinate your foods and grill them or broil on high.

Tarka (also **Baghaar** or **Chhaunk** or **Fodni**). A method of flavoring that is widely used in Indian cooking. (This is sometimes called *tempering* in Indian cuisine, though it is different from the tempering process in Western cuisine.) Spice-seasoned hot oil is added to flavor lightly cooked dishes. For more, see p. 23.

Tikka. Small pieces of chicken or paneer often skewered and broiled. Chicken Tikka Masala has now become part of British cuisine (the Empire strikes back).

Tofu (bean curd) is a soy product. Though high in protein and other nutrients, it is not in itself flavorful. Its texture allows it to absorb other flavors. Tofu comes from East Asia and is not traditionally used in India. Low in saturated fat; sometimes promoted as a substitute for paneer.

Toor (also **Tuvar** or **Arhar**). Called pigeon peas in English though you will not encounter that name when you shop for toor dal. Toor is a robust and popular dal, rich in protein. Famously used in both Rasam (p. 226) and Sambar (p. 125). See **Dals.**

Turmeric. A rhizome that looks somewhat like ginger but is very different in flavor and properties. Most often dried and powdered for use as a spice but can also be prepared fresh. Turmeric adds flavor and vibrant color. Use sparingly—a little goes a long way! Turmeric has been part of Indian cuisine and Hindu ritual since 1500 BCE and is permanently associated with Indian food. Its many medicinal and nutritional properties have long been recognized. According to a recent report from the American Cancer Society (2008), preliminary lab studies show that turmeric contains an antioxidant called curcumin, which is a powerful agent in fighting cancer. Further, in other scientific studies, turmeric has been shown to be a potential weapon against memory loss, specifically Alzheimer's disease (*The Journal of Biological Chemistry,* 2005).

Urad Dal. Sometimes referred to as *black gram.* A pale yellow dal with a thin black skin. Can be prepared with or without the skin. See **Dals.**

Vark (Edible Silver Leaf). Pure silver leaf, pounded so thin that it will crumble in your hands. Used to decorate festive foods, such as sweets, rice, or curries. The painstakingly hand-pounded film of silver is stored between layers of paper. When the foods are placed in serving platters, a sheet of paper bearing the gossamer-thin silver is gently inverted over the food and lightly pressed down so that the vark clings to the food. Store in airtight container or the silver will tarnish!

Vegetables, cooked. Although Indians enjoy uncooked vegetables in salads and raitas, cooked vegetables are often essential rather than side dishes. Cooked vegetables appear overdone to those not familiar with Indian cuisine. What you lose in color, you gain in taste. In Indian cooking, **Cauliflower** and **Cabbage** are often cooked very tender, almost mushy. If you prefer, leave them crunchy. **Okra** turns slimy when it is cut and comes in contact with water. To avoid this, after you wash the okra, be sure to dry it completely. Do not cook it in water. Add salt after the okra is well cooked. **Potatoes** are considered a vegetable and served with bread or rice.

White Poppy Seeds. Tiny white seeds. When ground, they thicken sauces and add texture to a gravy. Frequently used in vegetarian cooking. Roasting increases flavor.

Zafran. Same as **Saffron.** Has a delicate fragrance and adds a rich golden color to food. Used in sweet and savory dishes. Not to be confused with turmeric—which is also yellow-gold but is distinctly different in flavor and purpose.

Contributors

Indra Aggarwal ৺ Anupam Agrawal ৎ Shuchi Agrawal ৺ Pomila Ahuja ৎ Sowmya Anand ৎ P. R. Balgopal ৺ Shyamala Balgopal ৎ Manisha Bhagwat ৺ Krishna Bhowmik ৎ Shimmi Chandra ৺ Urmila Chandra ৎ Aradhna Chhajed ৺ Tulsi Dharmarajan ৎ Pradeep Dhillon ৺ Indranil Dutta ৎ Usha Gandhi ৺ Anita Goodnight ৎ Rajni Govindjee ৎ Hans Henrich Hock ৺ Zarina Hock ৎ Murtaza Husain ৺ Tasneem F. Husain ৎ Usha Jain ৺ Vijaya Jain ৎ Braj Kachru ৺ Yamuna Kachru ৎ Rashmi Kapoor ৺ Aruna Krishnamani ৎ Asha Kukreti ৺ Jaya Kumar ৎ Gullapudi Raman Kumari ৺ Ania Loomba ৎ Deepa Madhubalan ৺ Margrith Mistry ৎ Soli Mistry ৺ Nandini Pai ৎ Rajeshwari Pandharipande ৺ Annie Pawar ৎ Sujatha Purkayastha ৺ Aparna Rahman ৎ Vijaya Ramachandran ৺ Shantha Ranga Rao ৎ Kavitha Reddy ৺ Padma Reddy ৎ Munni Rodrigues ৺ Umeeta Sadarangani ৎ Anju Seth ৺ Pram Singh ৎ Zohreh Sullivan ৺ Vidya Tripathy ৎ Rajeswari Vanka ৺ Usha Yelamanchili ৎ Nancy Zutshi ৺

Recipe Index

314